QUESTIONABLE QUOKKAS

Coloring Book, Facts, & Games

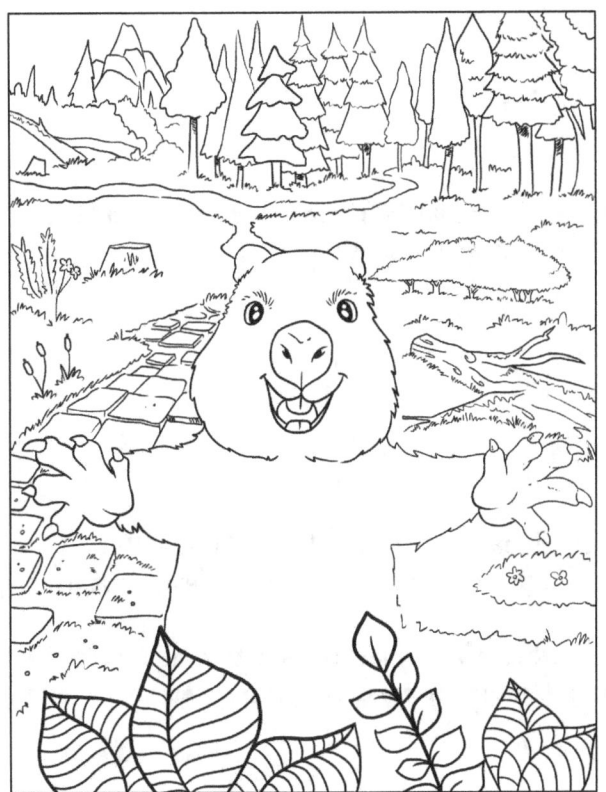

Dr. Jonathan Terry

Featuring

Illustrations by Desiree Albarran
Layout & Creative Mastery by Sarah Mugridge

Dr. Jonathan Terry
Walnut, CA
United States
2021

Questionable Quokkas

ISBN: 9798702434575

Proceeds from the sales of this coloring book may be used to fund mental health initiatives at the discretion of the editor. For more information, please visit www.mycapybara.com.

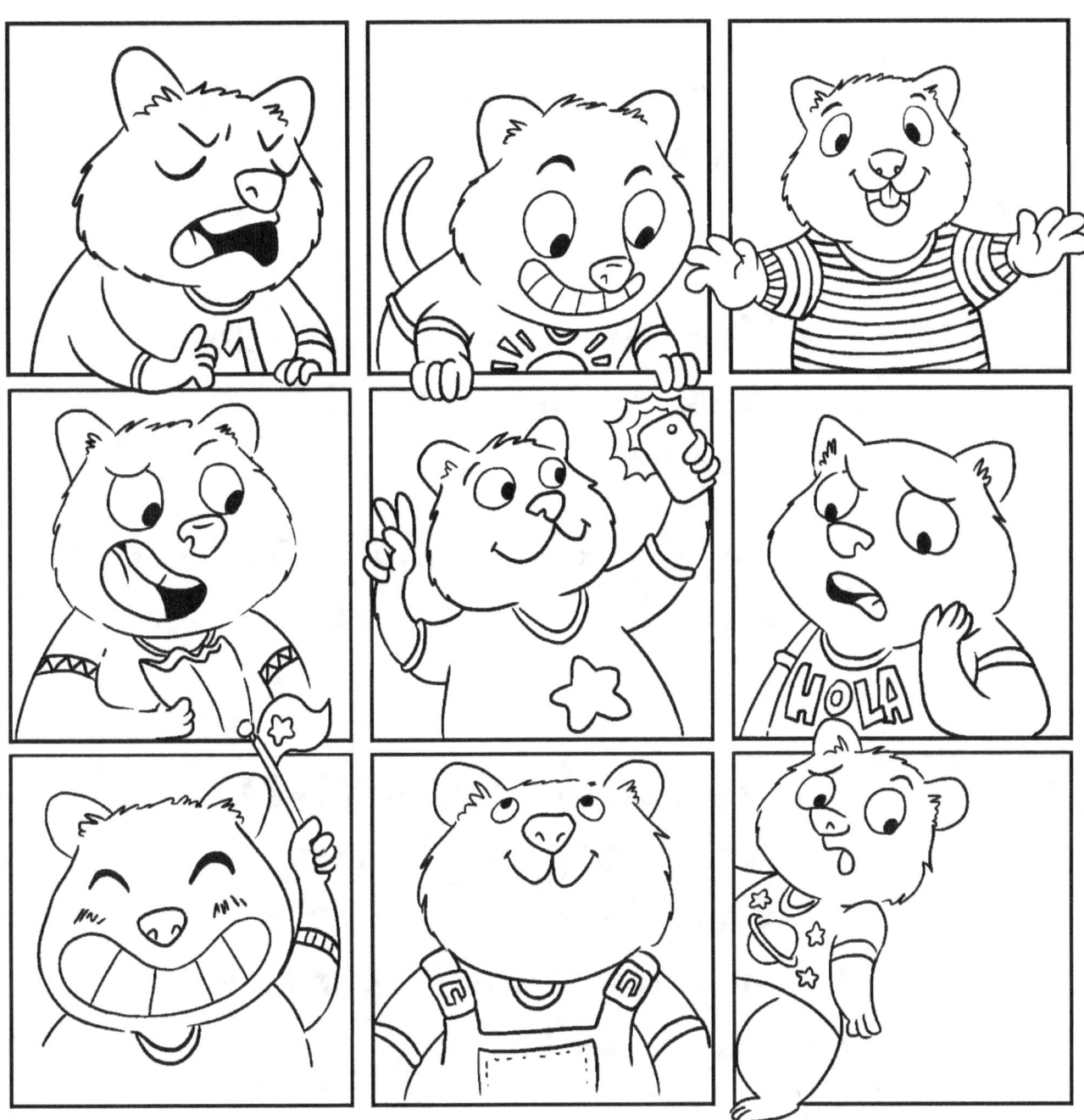

Have you even ever heard of a Quokka?

Well, let me tell you all about these *questionable* little creatures.

Quokkas are generally the size of a domestic cat.

Their bodies can be 15-21 inches long (39-54 cm), while their tails can be anywhere from 9-12 inches (23-31 cm).

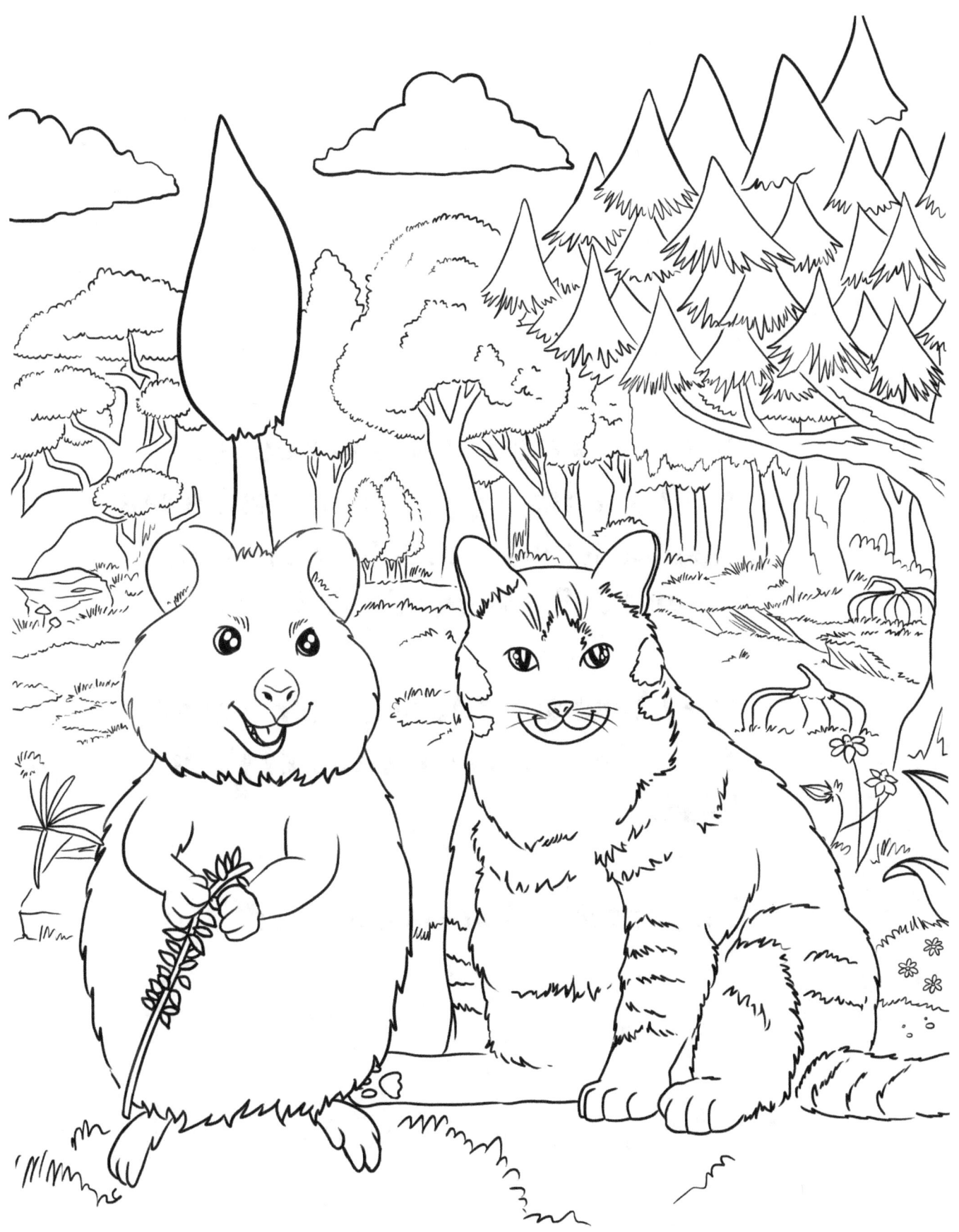

Male quokkas can weigh between 5-10 pounds (2.2-4.5kg), while the smaller females usually weigh in around 3-8 pounds (1.4-3.6kg).

They have short faces, short tails and round ears at the top of their head.

Talk about cuteness overload!

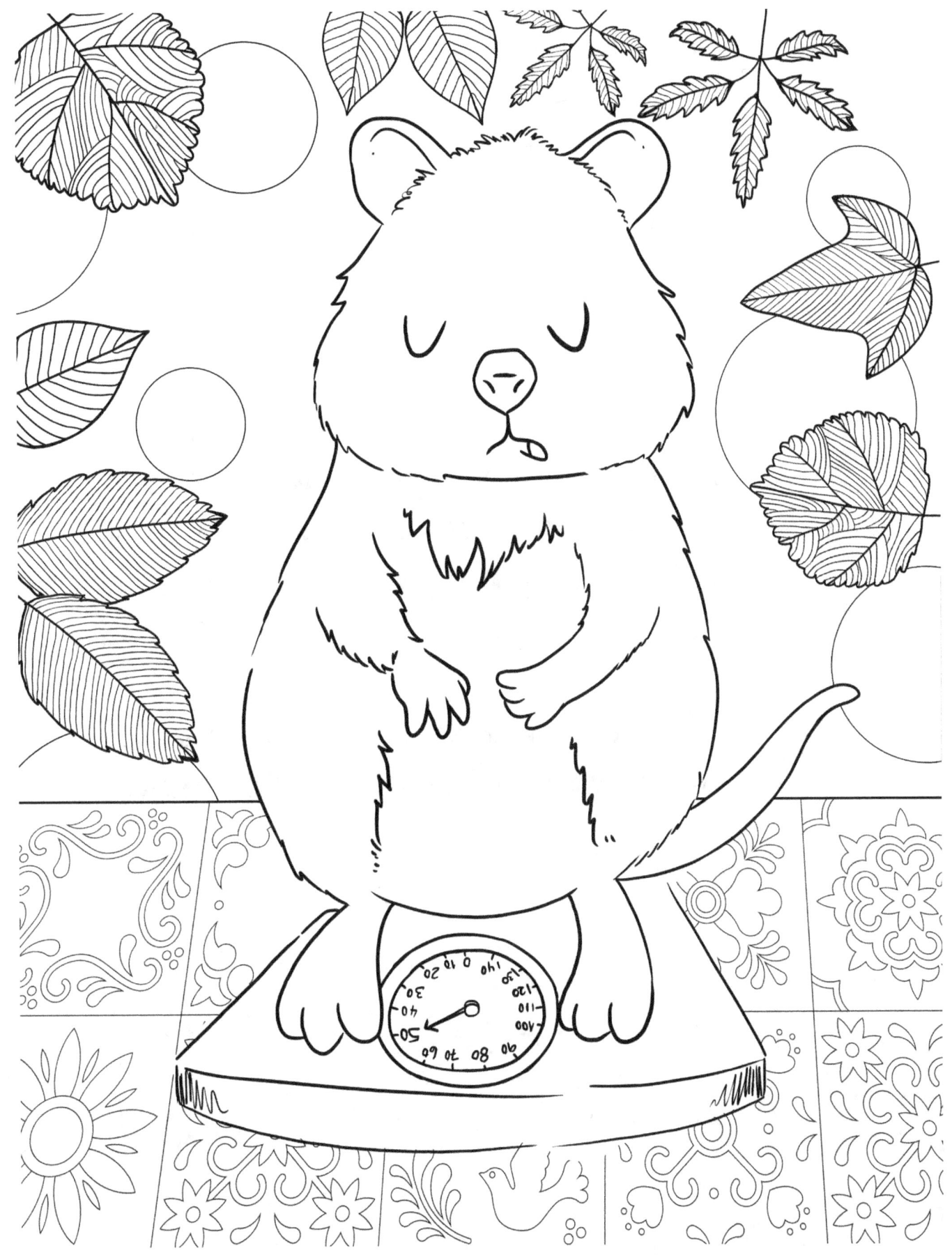

The Quokka has a perpetual smile, which is why this cutie has been named the happiest animal on earth!

All that happiness... It really makes you question what they're thinking.

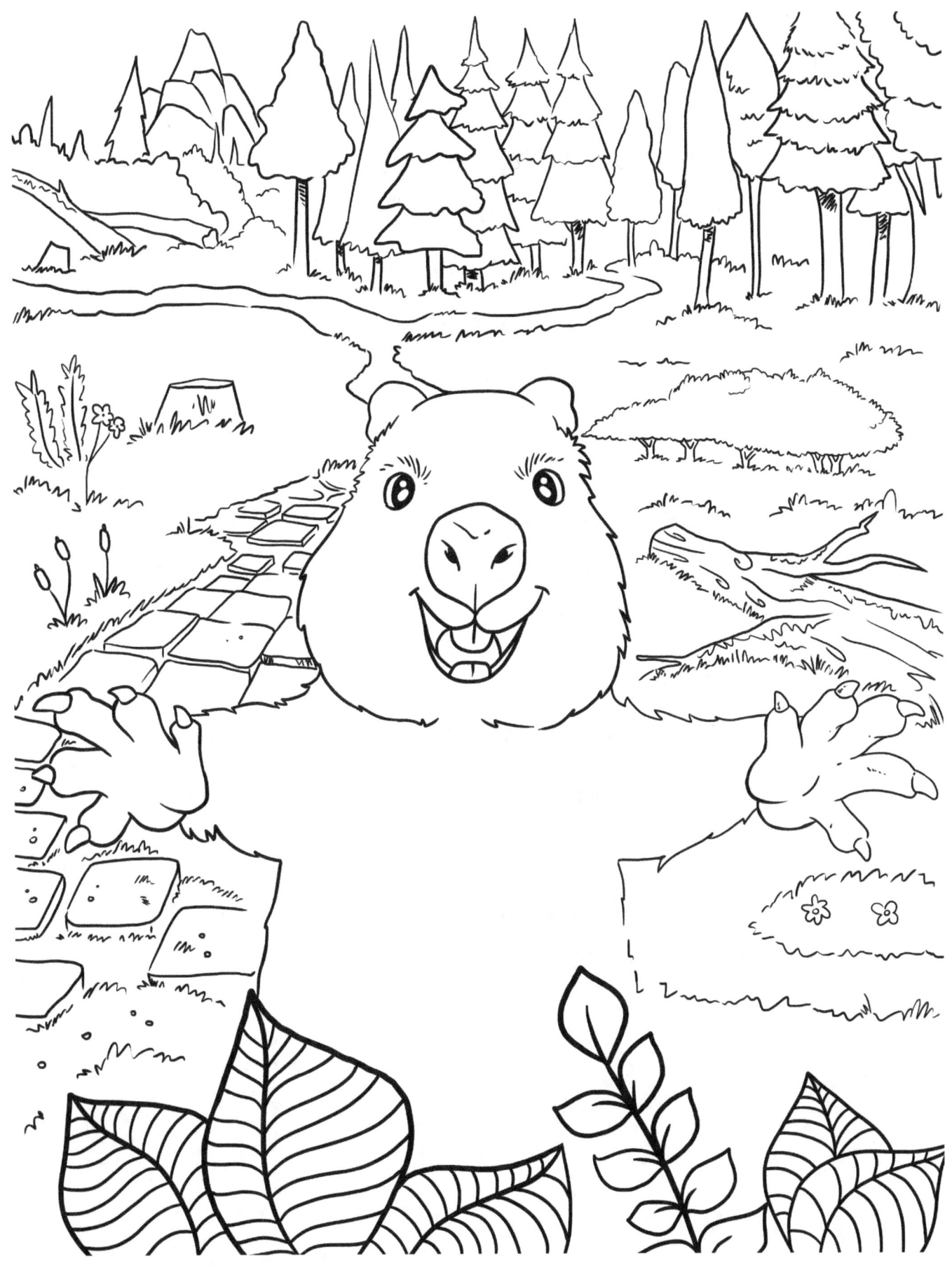

A quokka by any other name would be just as cute! The quokka goes by many names, including the short-tailed wallaby, Ban-gup, Bungeup, Quak-a, and Fred.

Don't be fooled by the spelling: the quokka's name is pronounced *Kwaa-Kaa.*

Turn to someone near you and practice saying that: *Kwaa-Kaa!*

See if you can get them to say it back: *Kwaa-Kaa!*

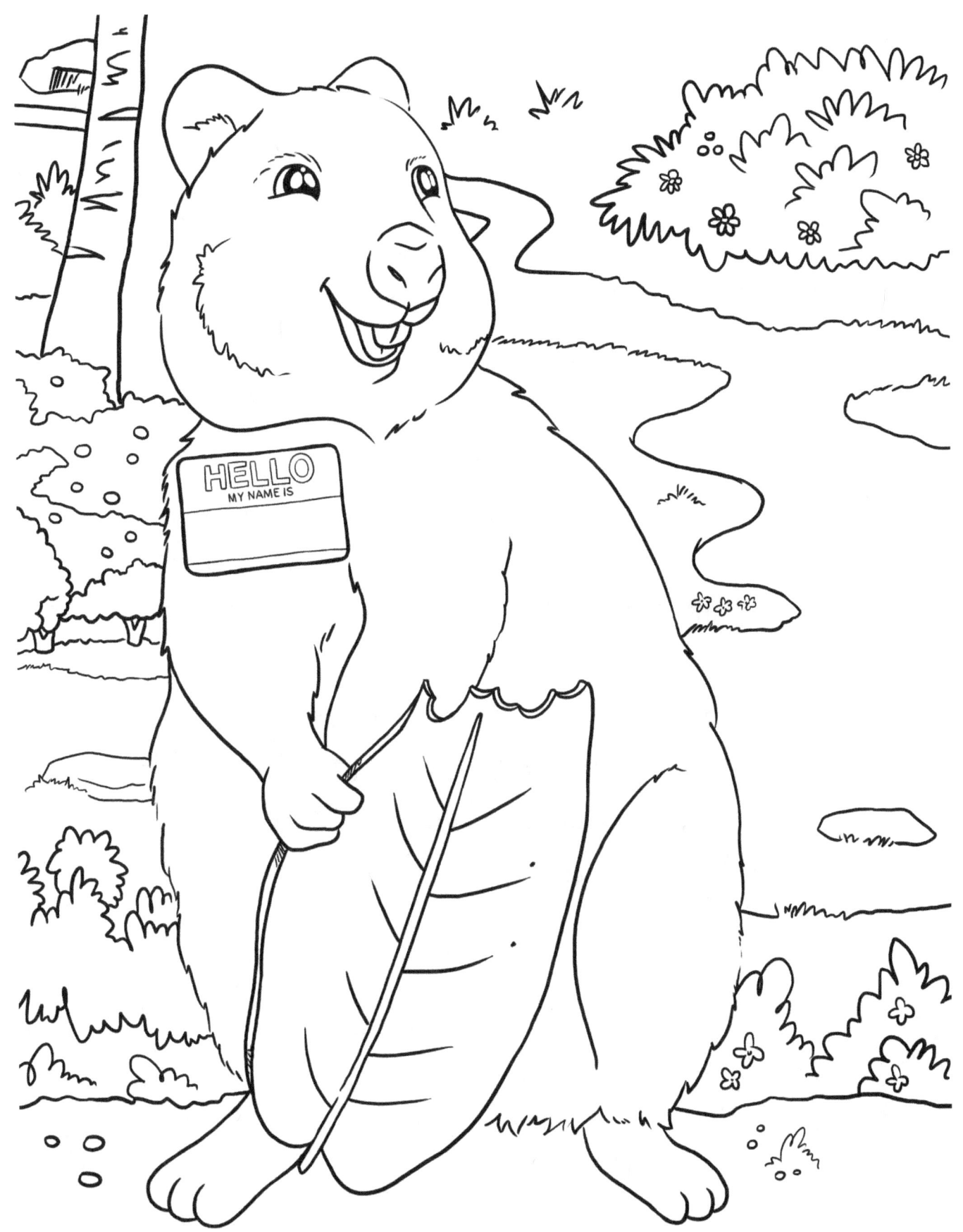

Despite what you might think, quokkas don't quack.

In fact, they have very little in common with ducks.

Quokkas prefer peace and quiet.

However, quokkas in captivity in zoos have been known to make a lot of noise during feeding time. Sort of like ringing a quokka dinner bell!

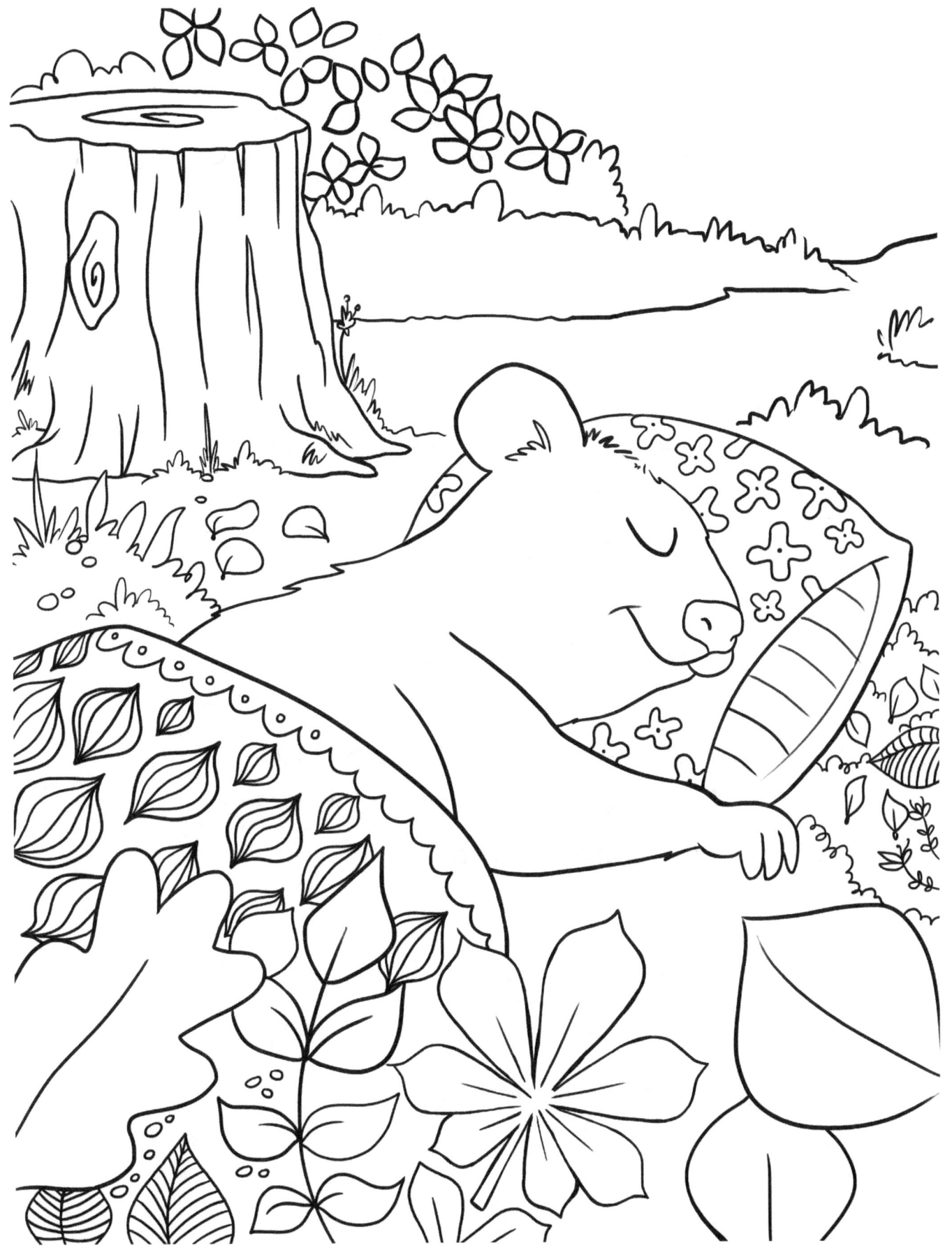

Quokkas are generally found in the South-western region of Australia, Mate!

First identified by Dutch explorers, quokkas can also be found on Rottnest and Bald Islands in the forests, swamps, and coastal plains.

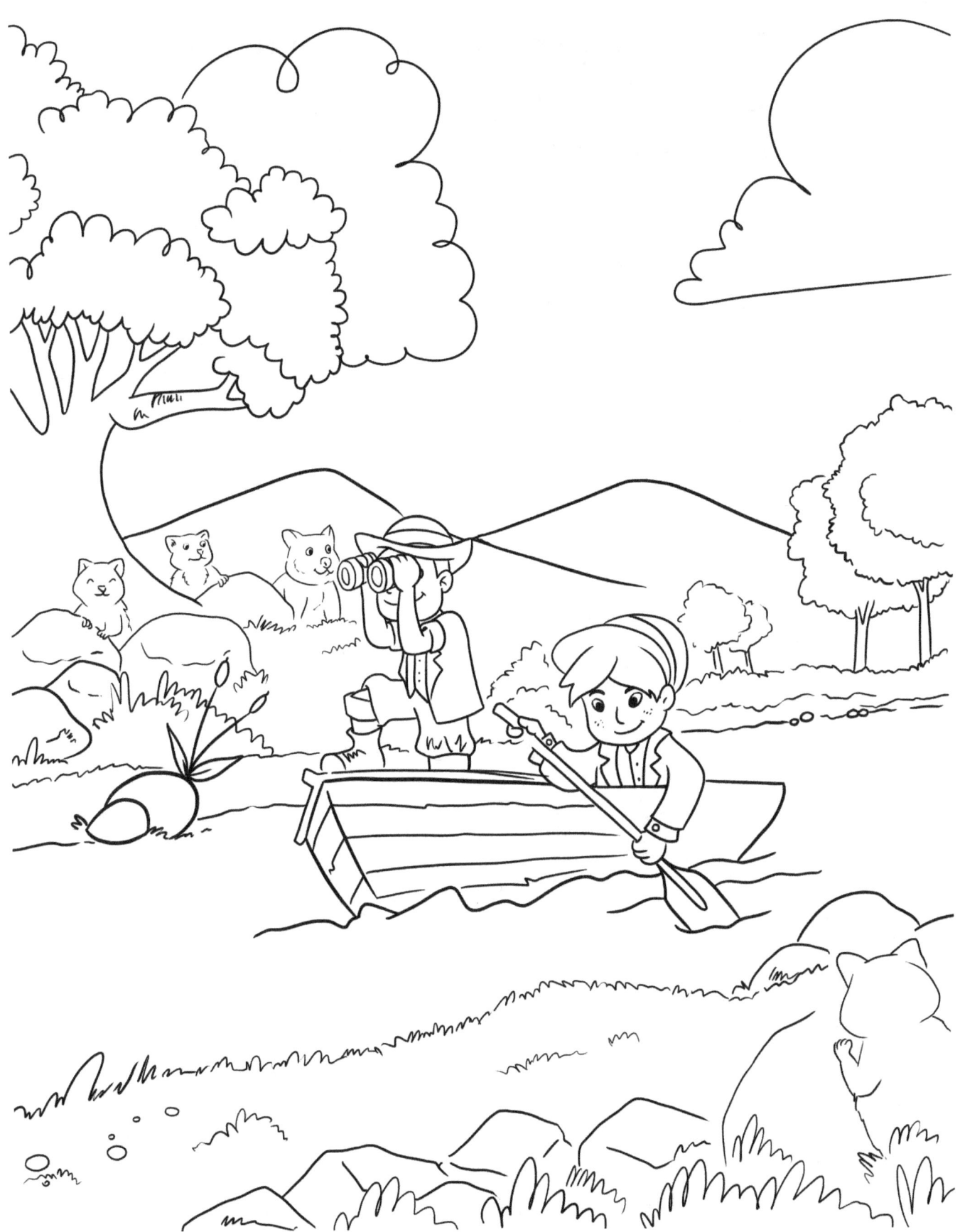

When European explorers first saw the quokka, they thought he was a very large rat! How rude!

Very large rats are covered in two of our other books.

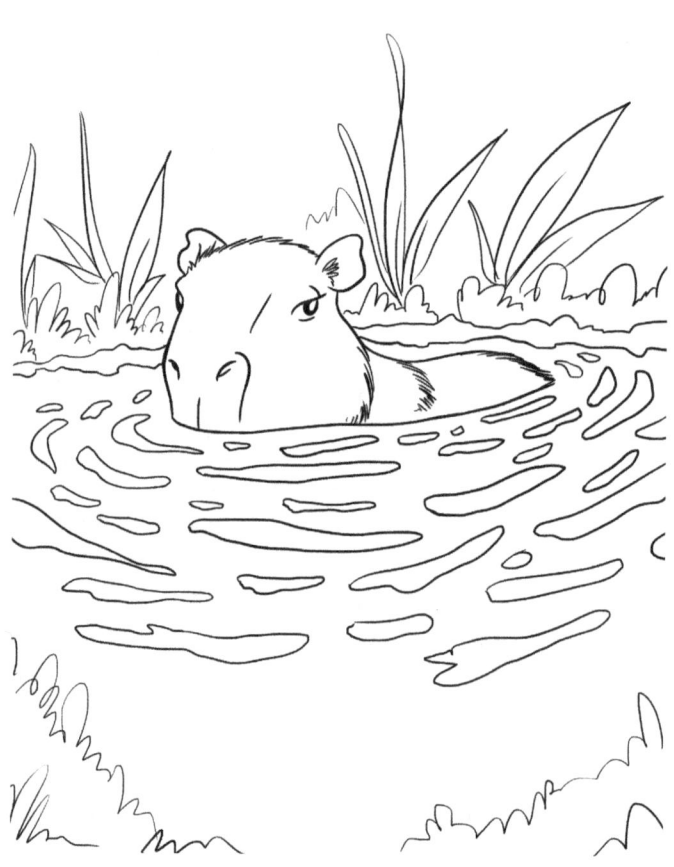

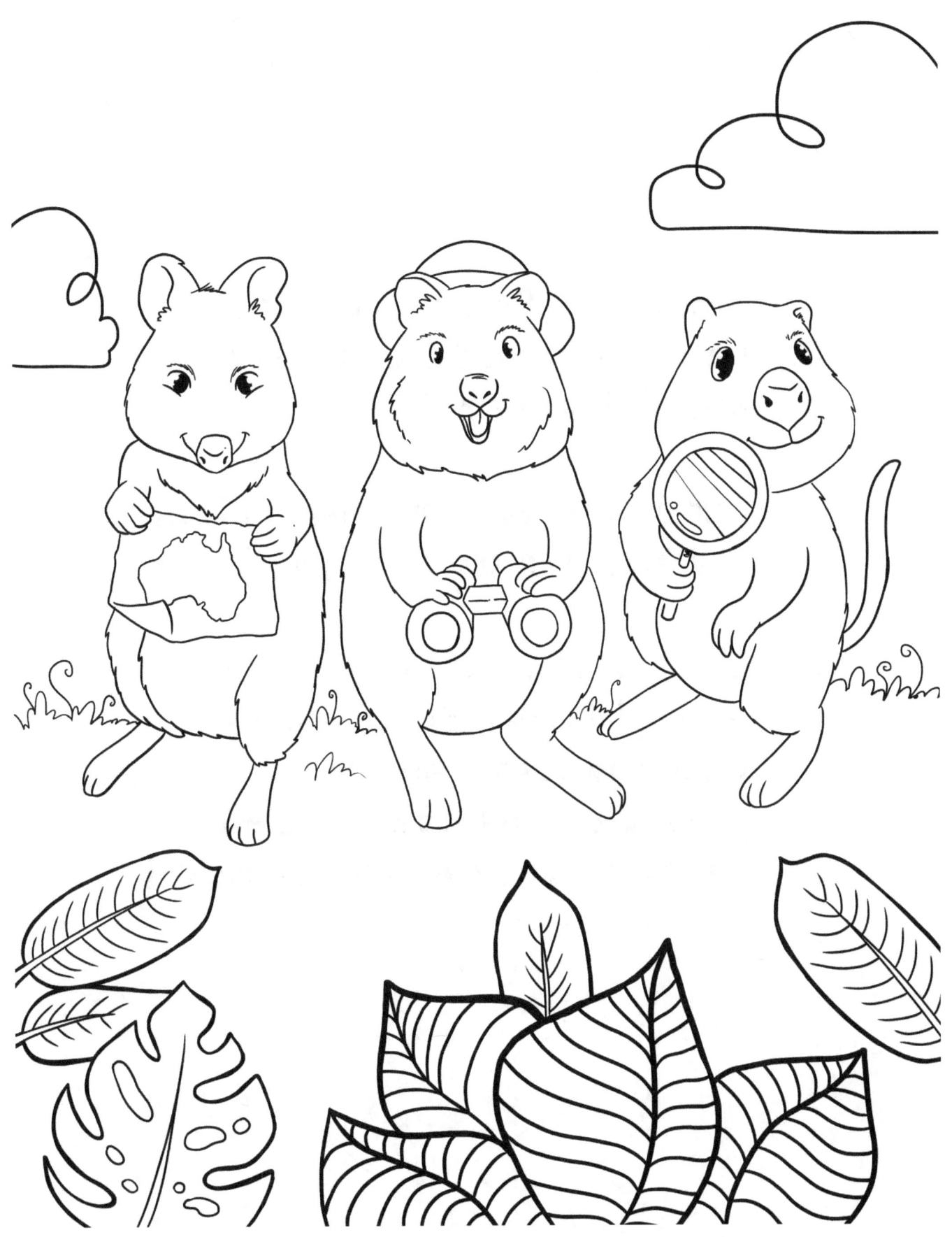

Rottnest, or "rat's nest" Island may have been named after the quokka, but she is not a rodent!

Quokkas are actually small wallabies and belong to the marsupial family.

Other members of the marvelous marsupial clan include kangaroos, tree-kangaroos, wallaroos, pademelons, wallabies, and even our friend the Impossible Opossum!

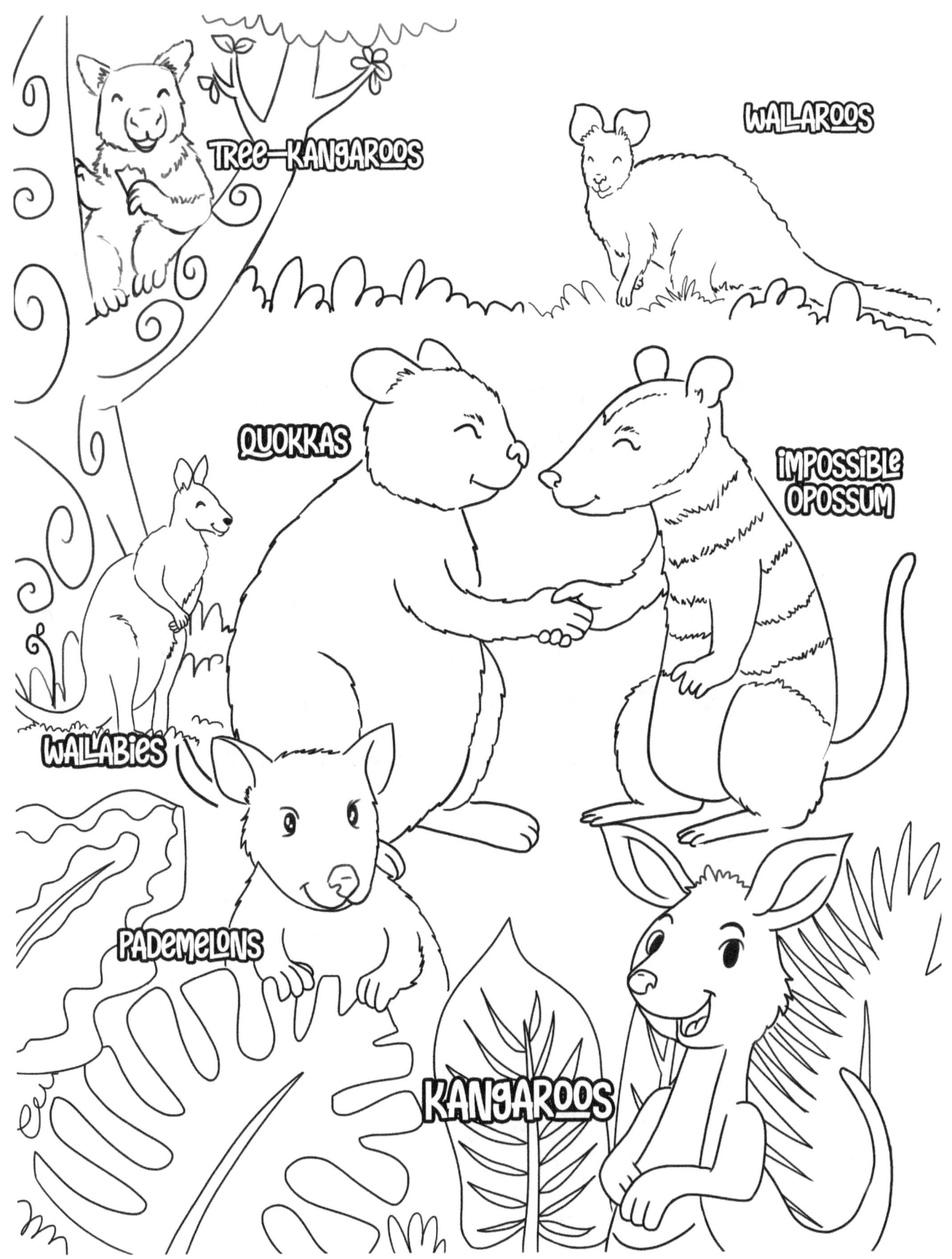

Mainland Australian quokkas can look very different from their island brothers.

All quokkas are known for their coarse, thick greyish-brown fur, but some Rottnest and mainland quokkas come in a range of shades.

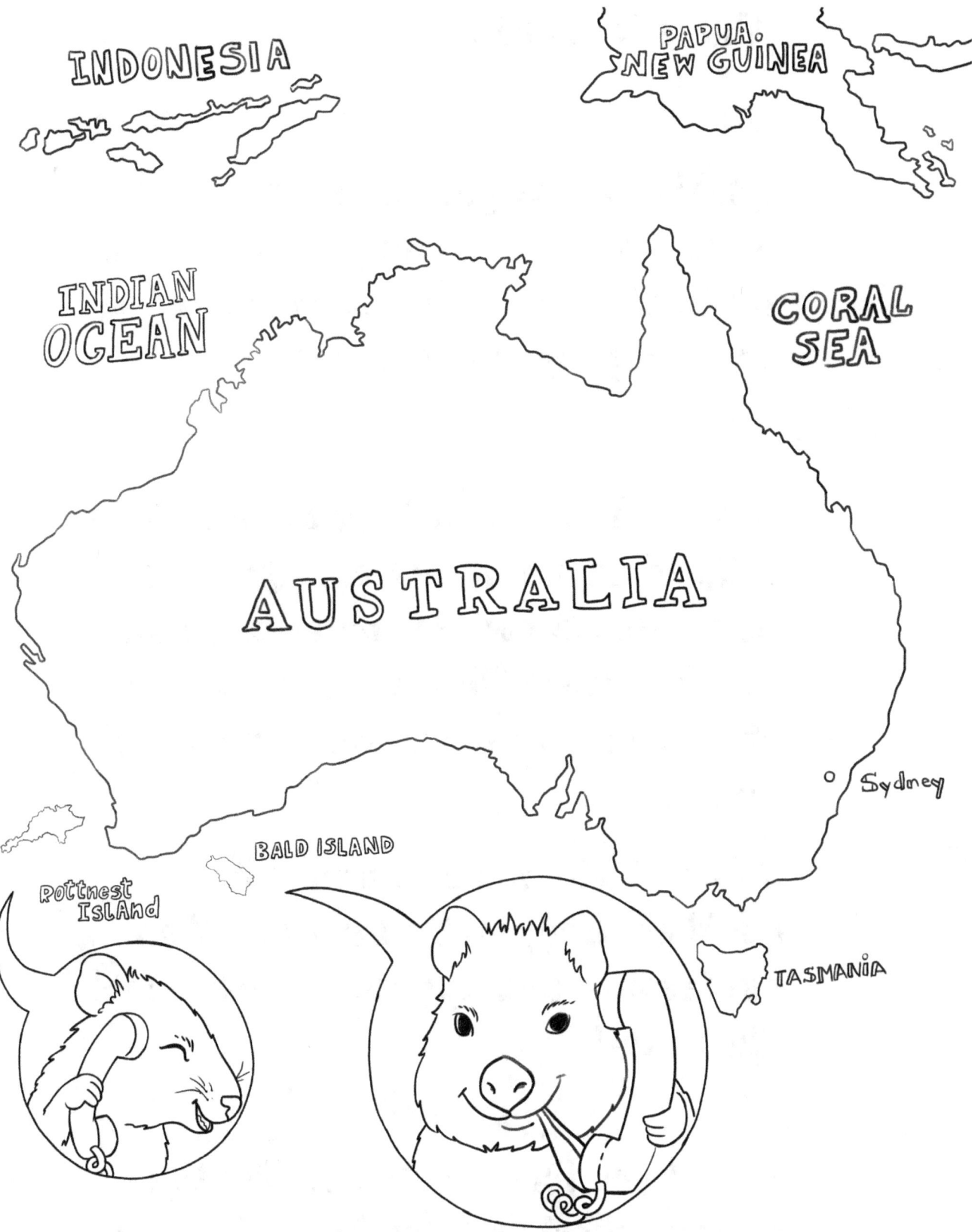

What's for lunch?

Quokkas are vegetarians, or herbivores. They enjoy a good salad made of leaves, shrubs, yummy bark, and many types of grasses.

But don't turn your back on this cheeky fella while you're eating. Quokkas have been known to snatch an extra snack or two. Who could be mad at that face? I would totally give her a snack!

Oh - and who's that dining with the quokka? Why, that's *Desiree Albarran*, our favorite and <u>not at all</u> questionable illustrator!

P.S. If you like vegetables like the quokka, check out our first children's book and coloring book, *Eat the Rainbow.*

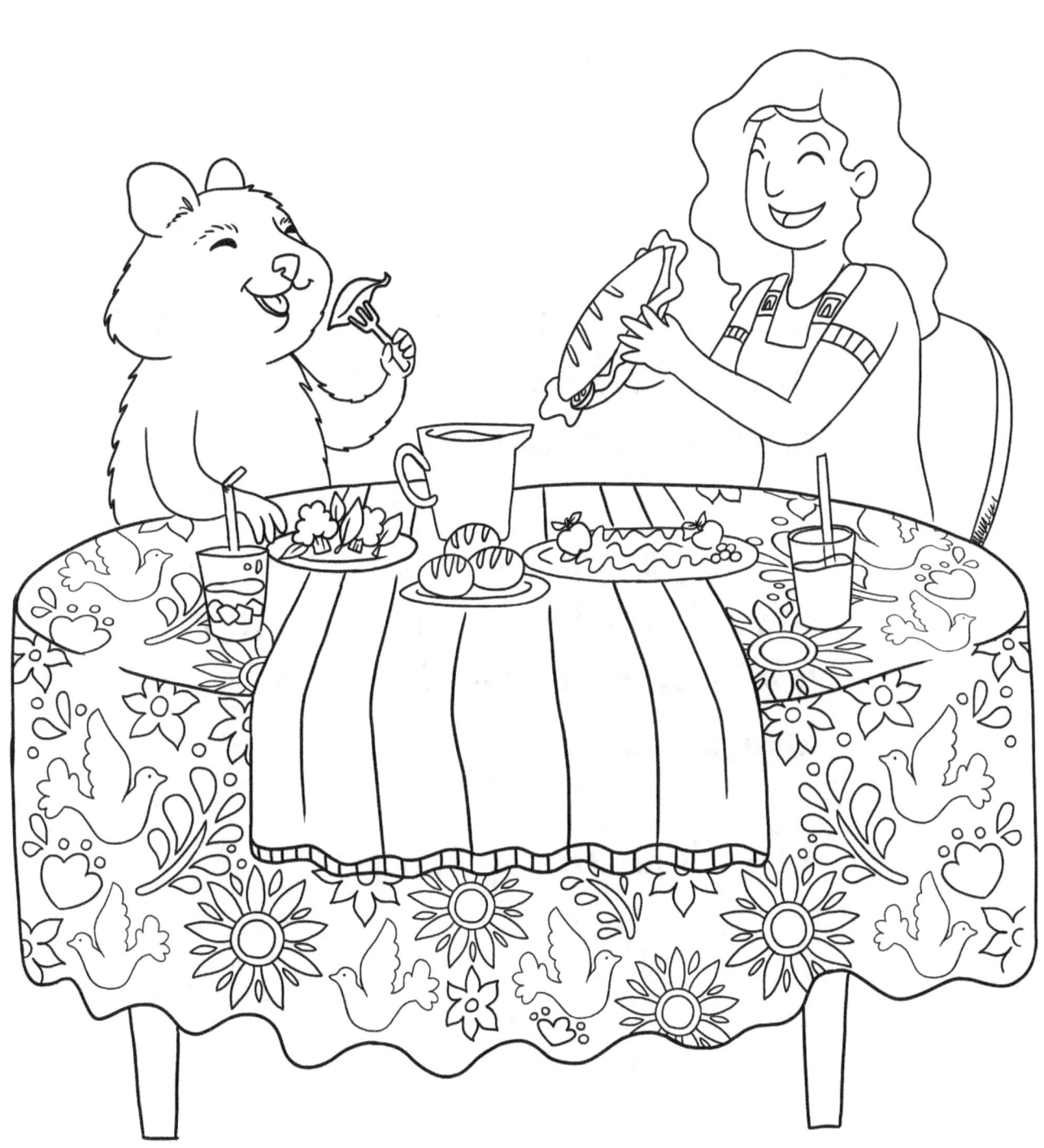

Like other marsupials, quokkas carry their babies, or *joeys* in an abdominal pouch.

The impossible opossums in our other book do this, too - though you might be more familiar with kangaroos.

Talk about riding in style!

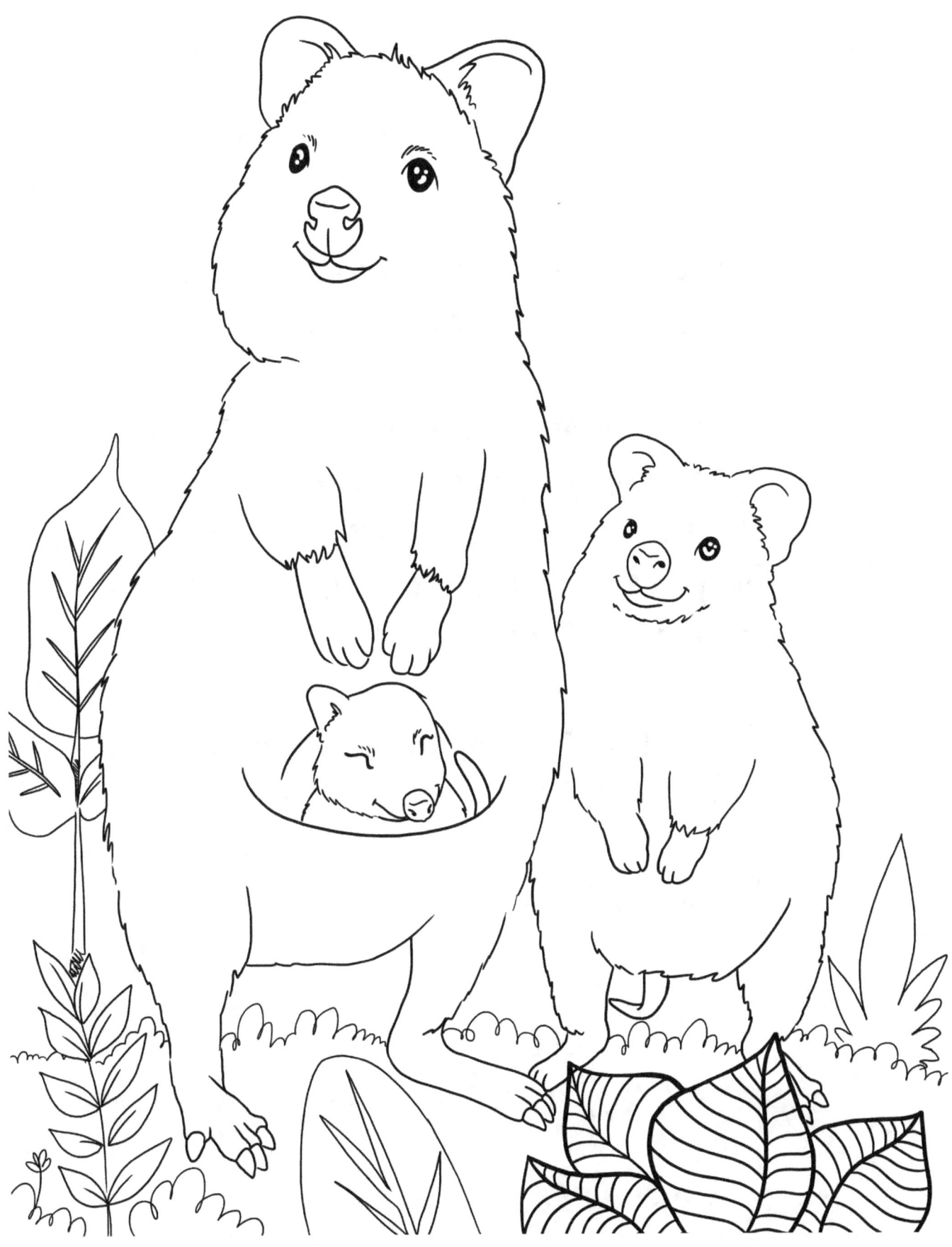

Quokkas aren't likely to earn any Parent of the Year awards.

Quokka fathers have no involvement in raising the joeys, and quokka mothers have been known to use their joeys as a distraction to get away from predators.

This type of behavior is discouraged in humans.

Seriously.

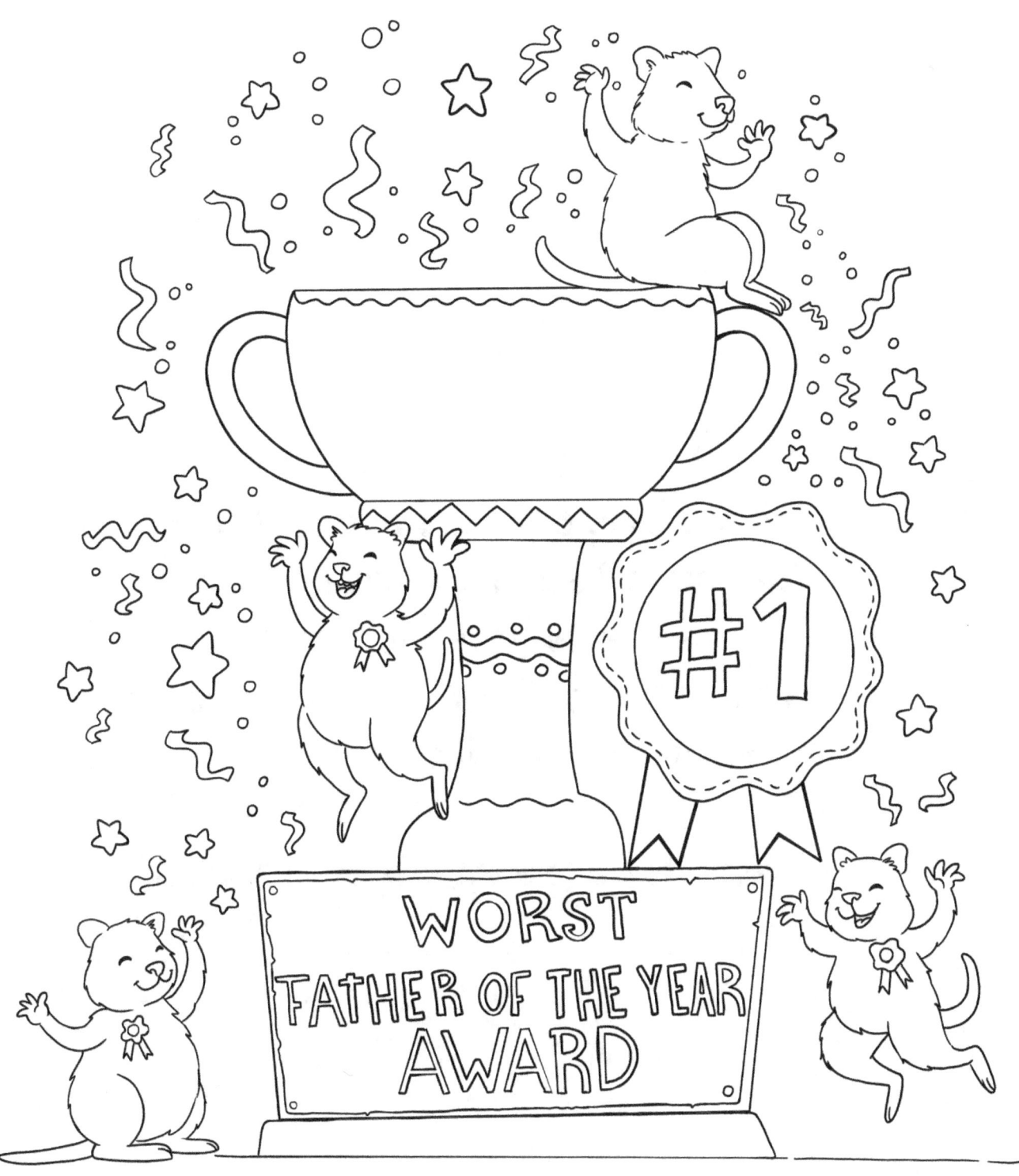

As cute and cuddly as our little friends are, quokkas are protected by the Australian government, and overly-affectionate visitors can be fined up to $300 or even receive jail time just for petting them.

I repeat, *back away from the quokka.*

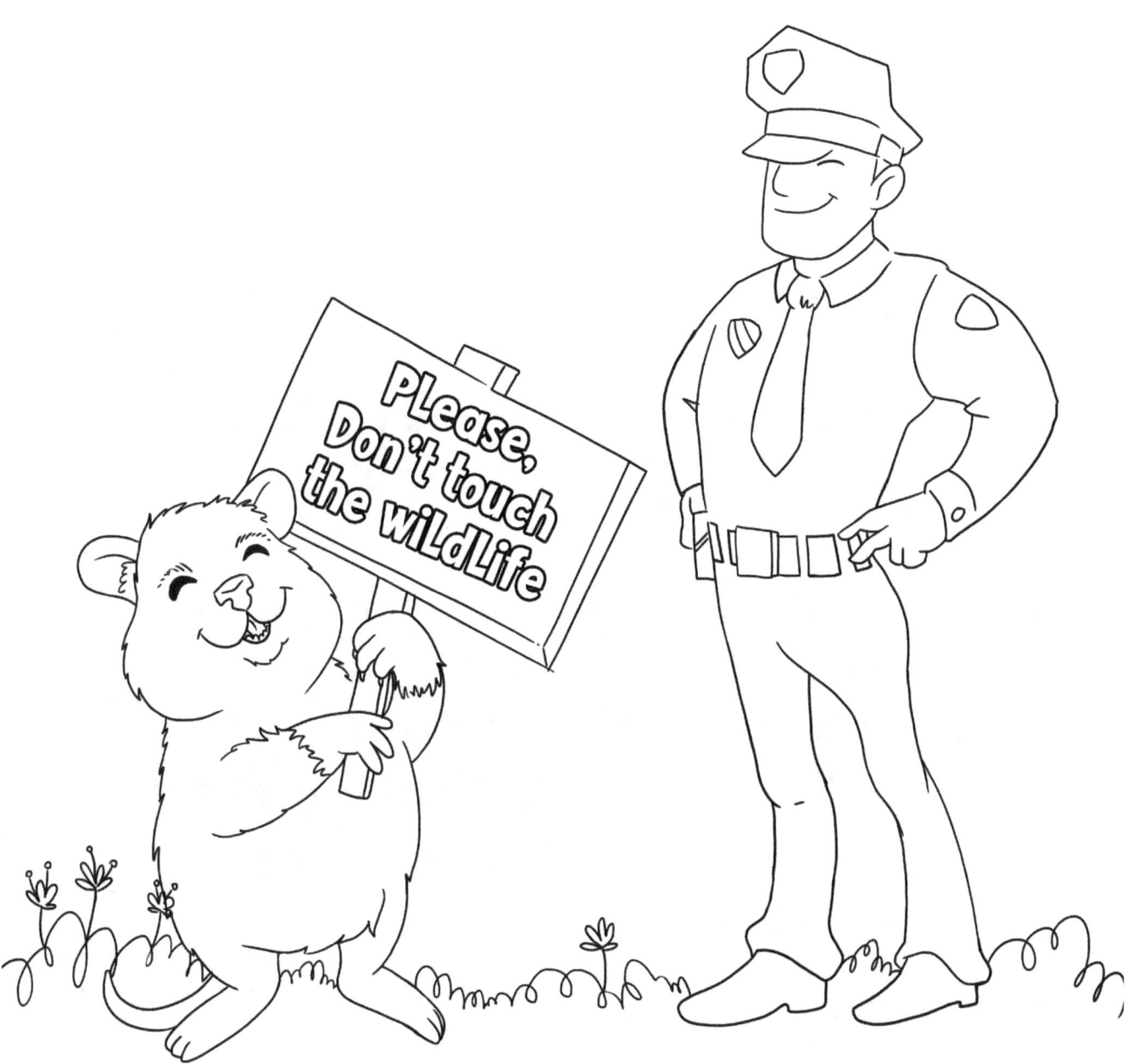

Once a thriving species, the quokka population is considered a threatened species, and likely to become extinct in the wild.

Do you remember the endangered animal we've covered in another coloring book? If you said the RED PANDAS from *Red, White, and Panda*, your answer is stu-panda-ously correct!

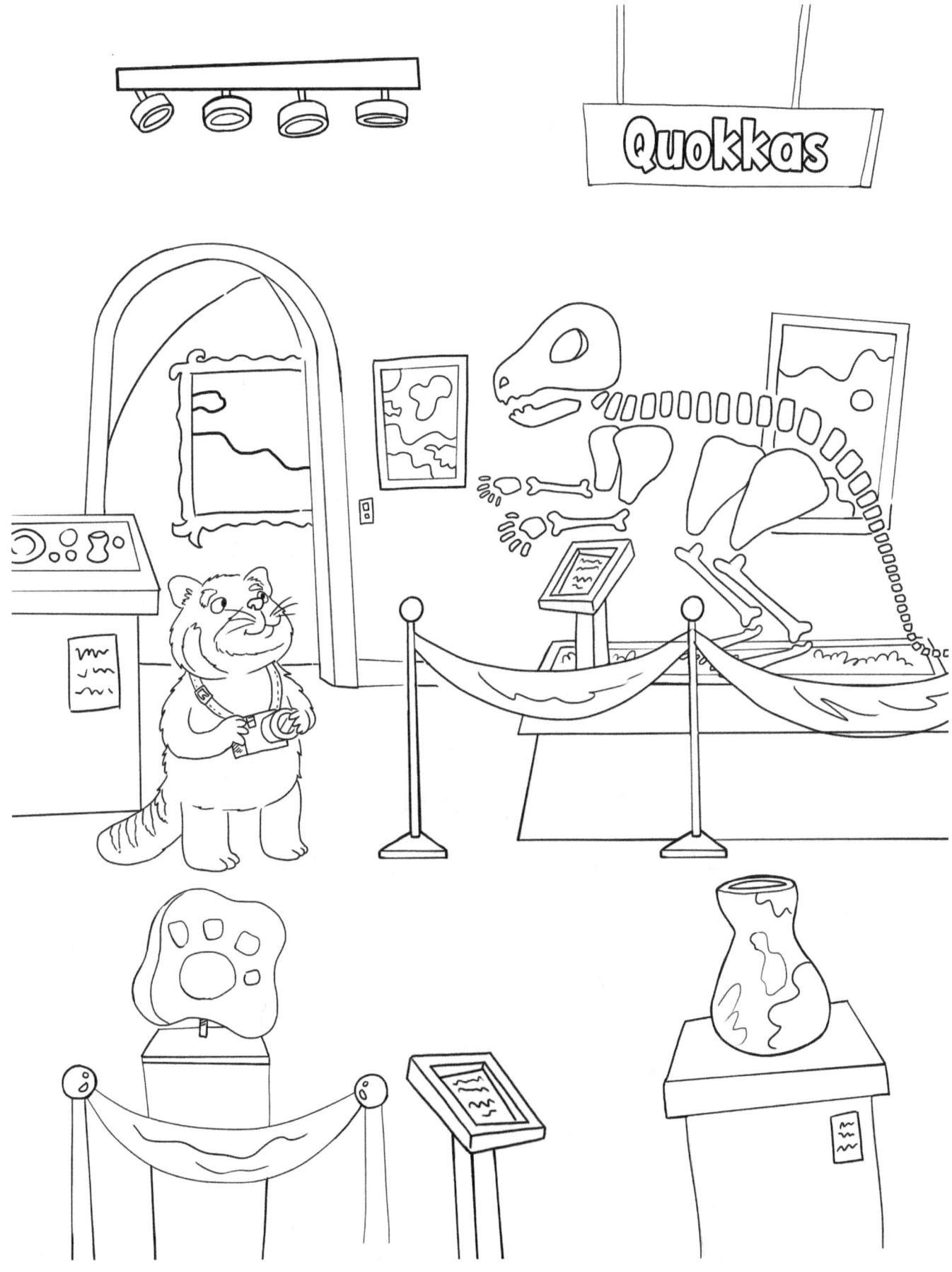

Never mind raining cats and dogs, it's raining quokkas and…quokkas!

The dwindling mainland population of quokkas is located in areas with heavy rainfall.

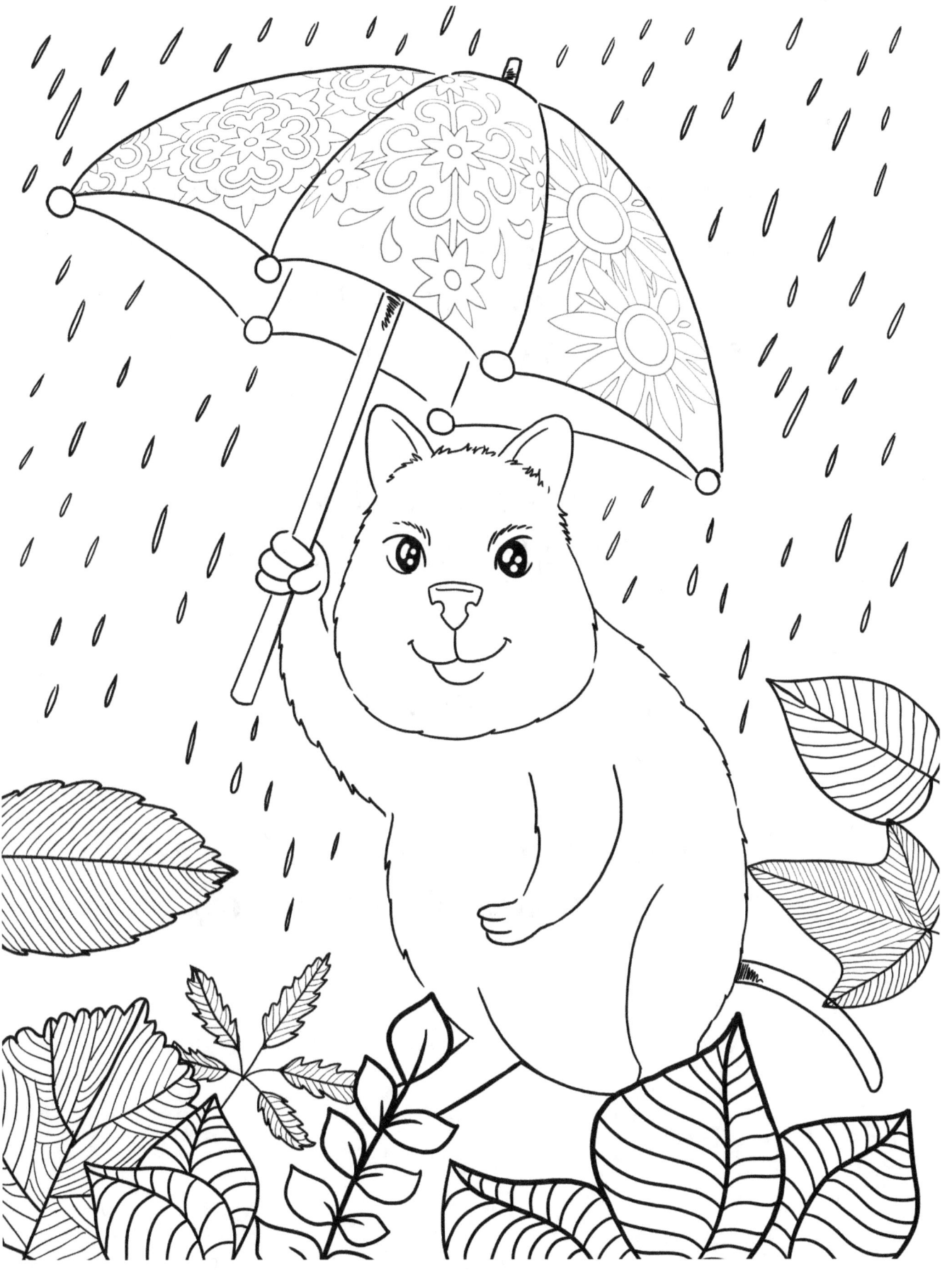

The scientific name for the quokka is *Setonix brachyurus*. "Brachyurus" is loosely borrowed from the Greek term for *short tail*, brakhús.

While here, do you know what a quokka's favorite holiday is?

I heard it's Qu-onukkah!

(And also wishing a happy Qu-anzaa to all our friends who celebrate!)

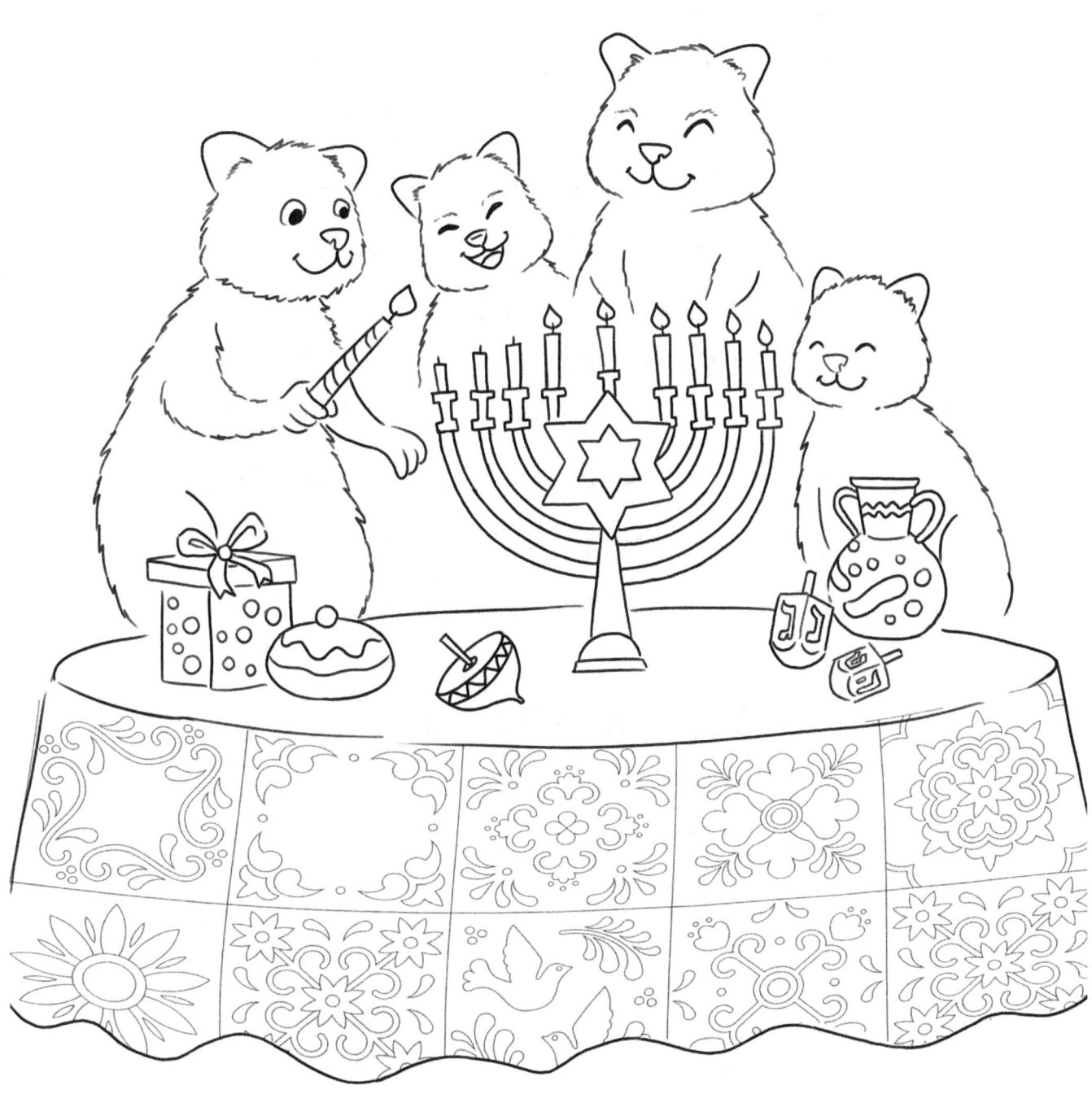

Many animals pose a threat to the quokka on the mainland, including foxes, birds of prey, snakes, dingoes, and domestic animals like dogs and cats. Can you guess which animal poses the biggest threat? You guessed it... Humans!

Pictured here are Sarah and Terry who helped with the research and layout for this book.

LADIES, seriously, put DOWN the quokkas. They are not for playing!

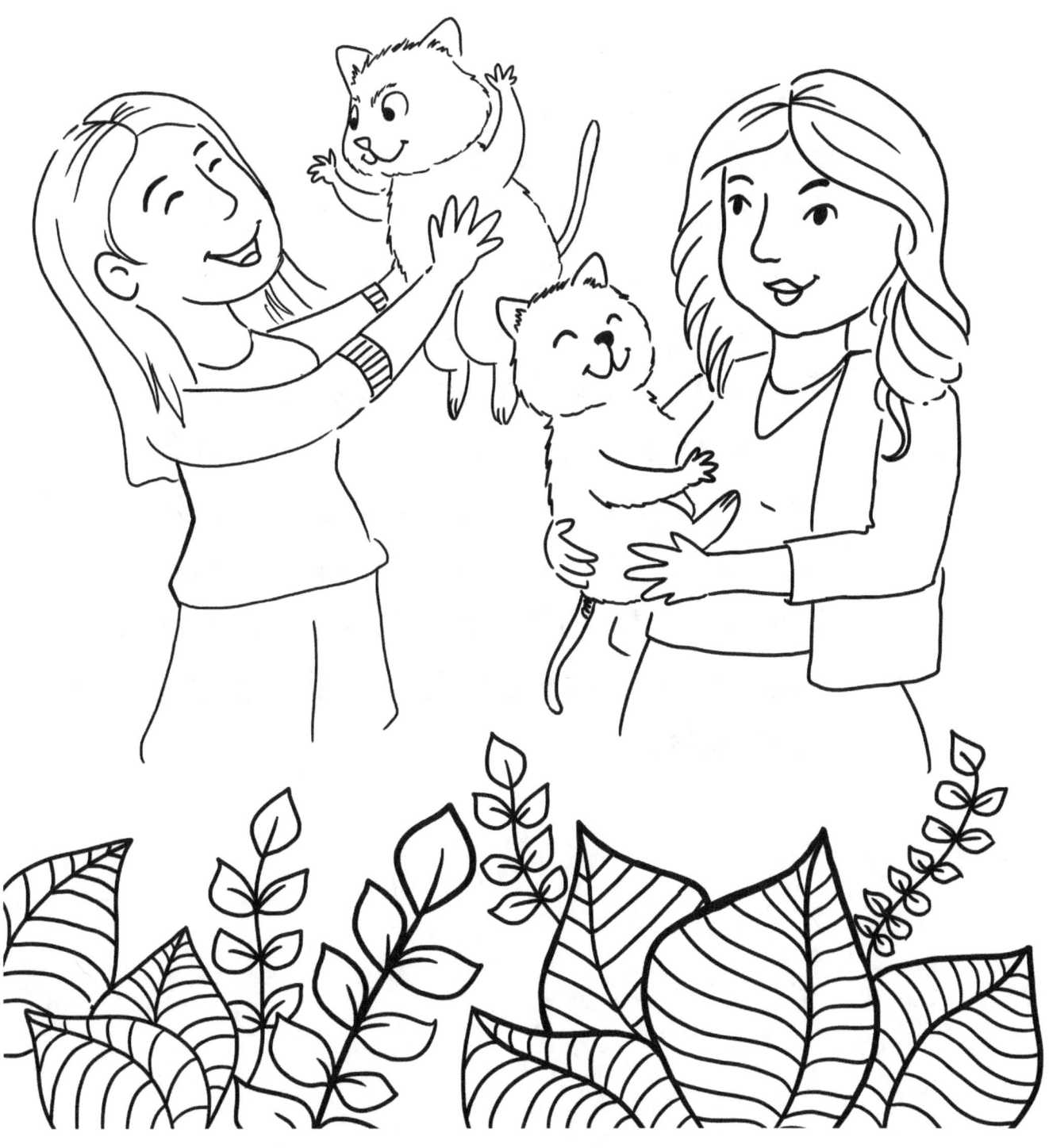

Deforestation poses the most significant threat to quokkas, followed closely by severe weather changes and climate change.

The 2015 wildfire that decimated much of Western Australian wildlife reduced the local quokka population by 90%. We hope that learning to love quokkas like we do will convince you to help protect these little guys and gals!

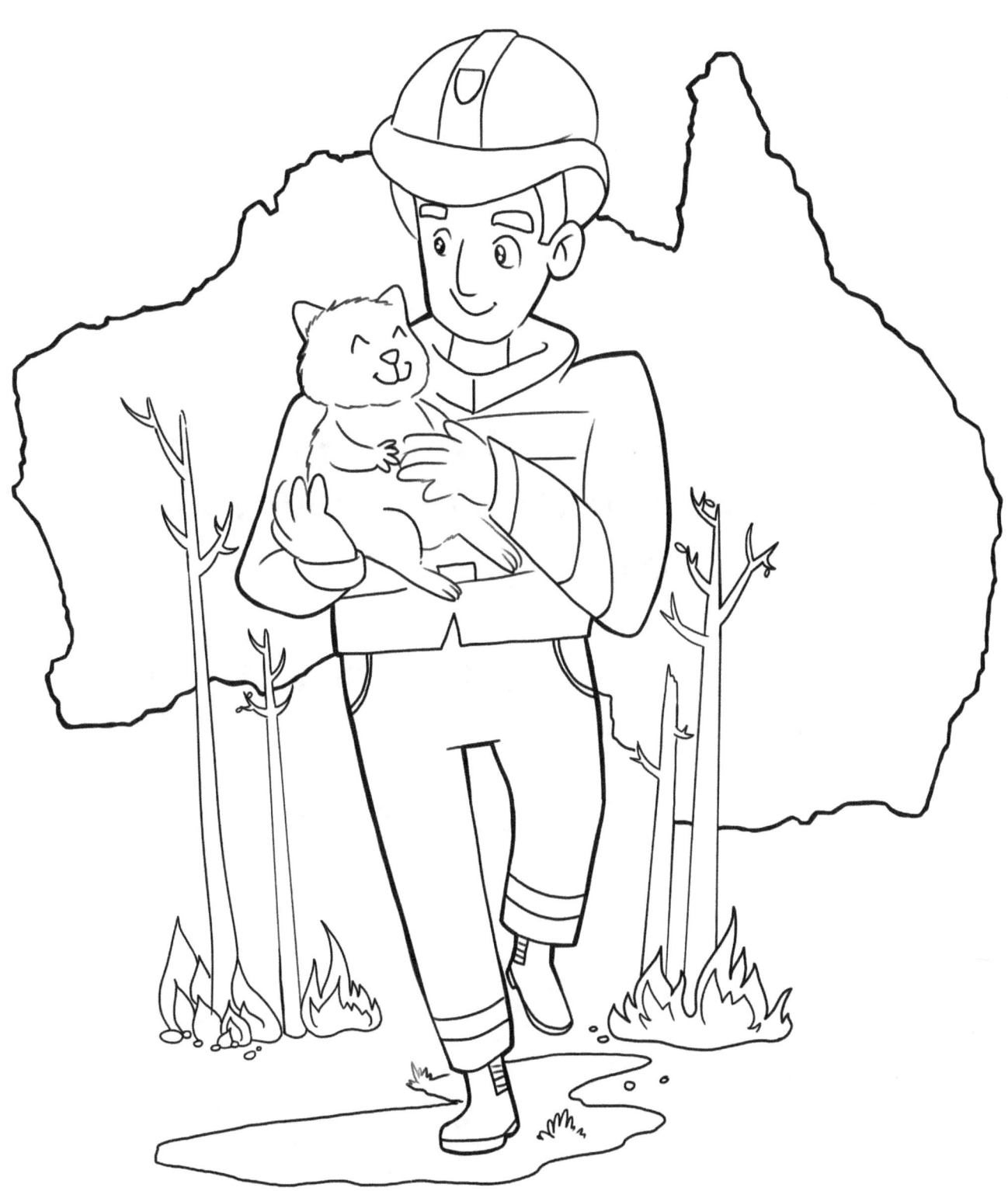

Luckily, quokkas have no natural predators on Rottnest Island and live long, happy lives.

Living there isn't the rottenest, now, after all.

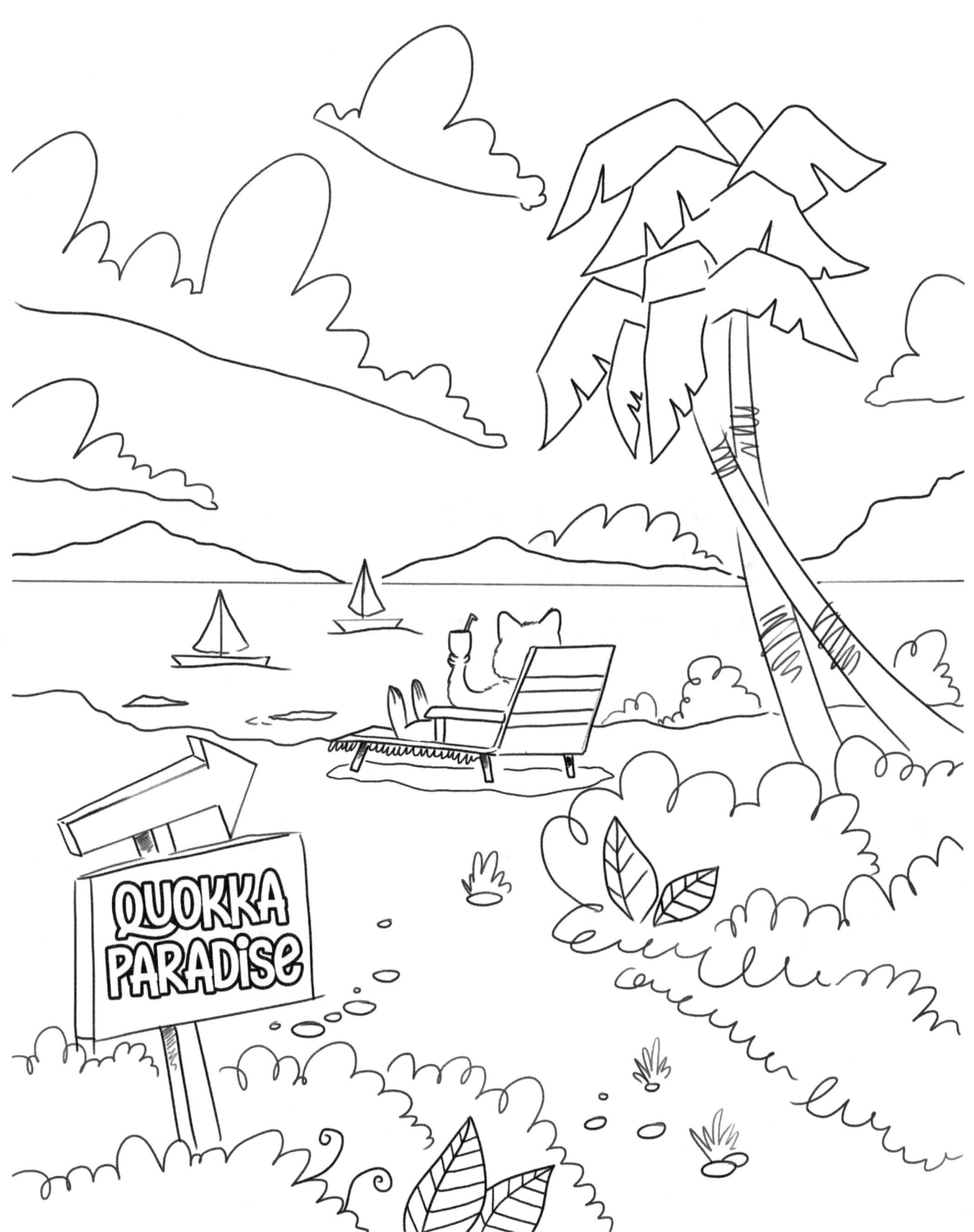

A picture says a thousand words! The quokka's toothy grin makes him an awesome selfie partner.

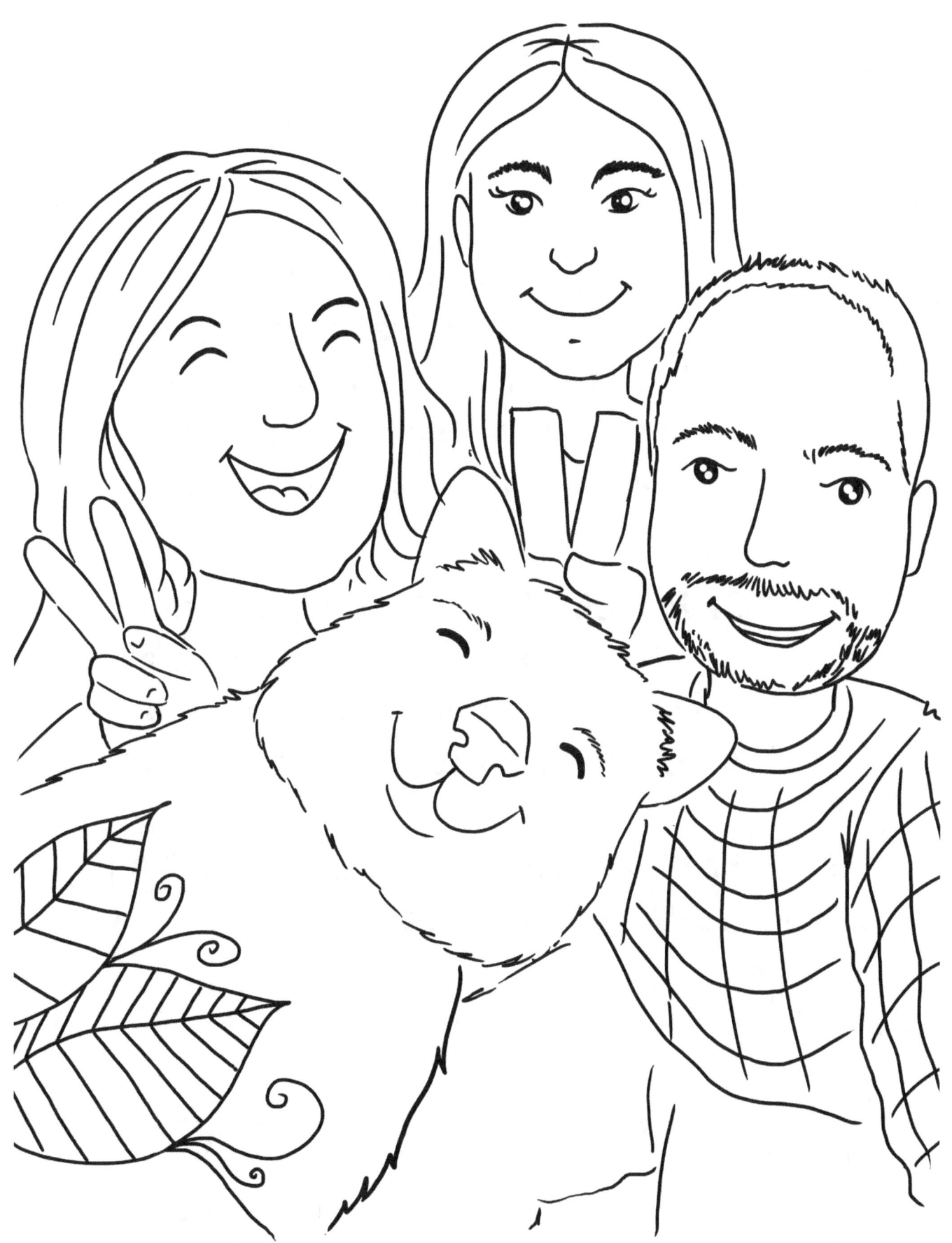

In fact, the popularity of quokka selfies in recent years has increased global awareness of this threatened population and helped raise funds to support environmental protections.

Selfies with this coloring book are *also* highly encouraged and not at all questionable. Please send them to us and share on social media!!

See if you can spot the quokka taking a selfie on our shiny book cover.

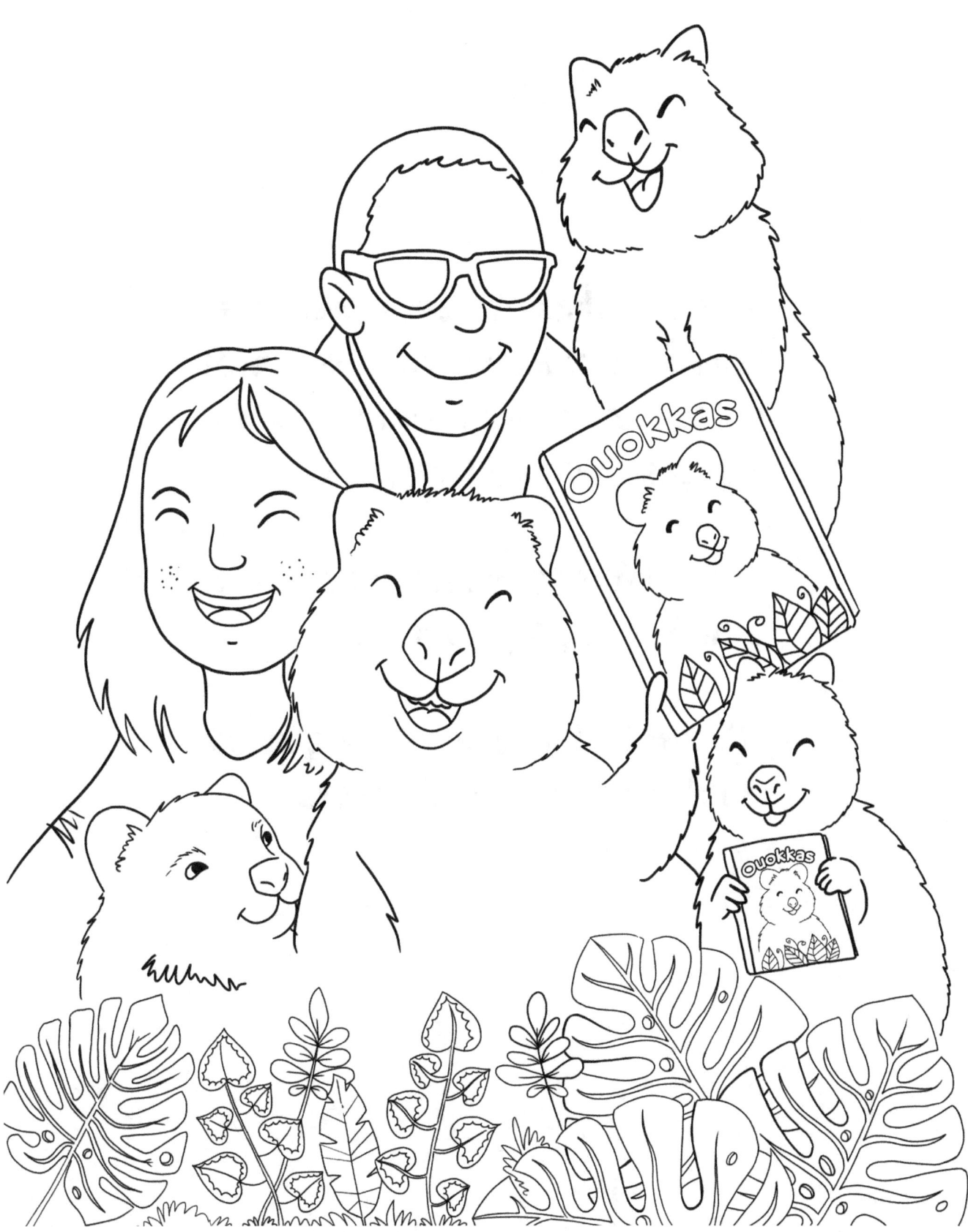

Two quokkas are cute, but three's a crowd. Quokkas live in colonies for safety and mating purposes, but typically live solitary lives.

They don't typically groom one another or play together.

It's probably safe to say quokkas don't like to play checkers...

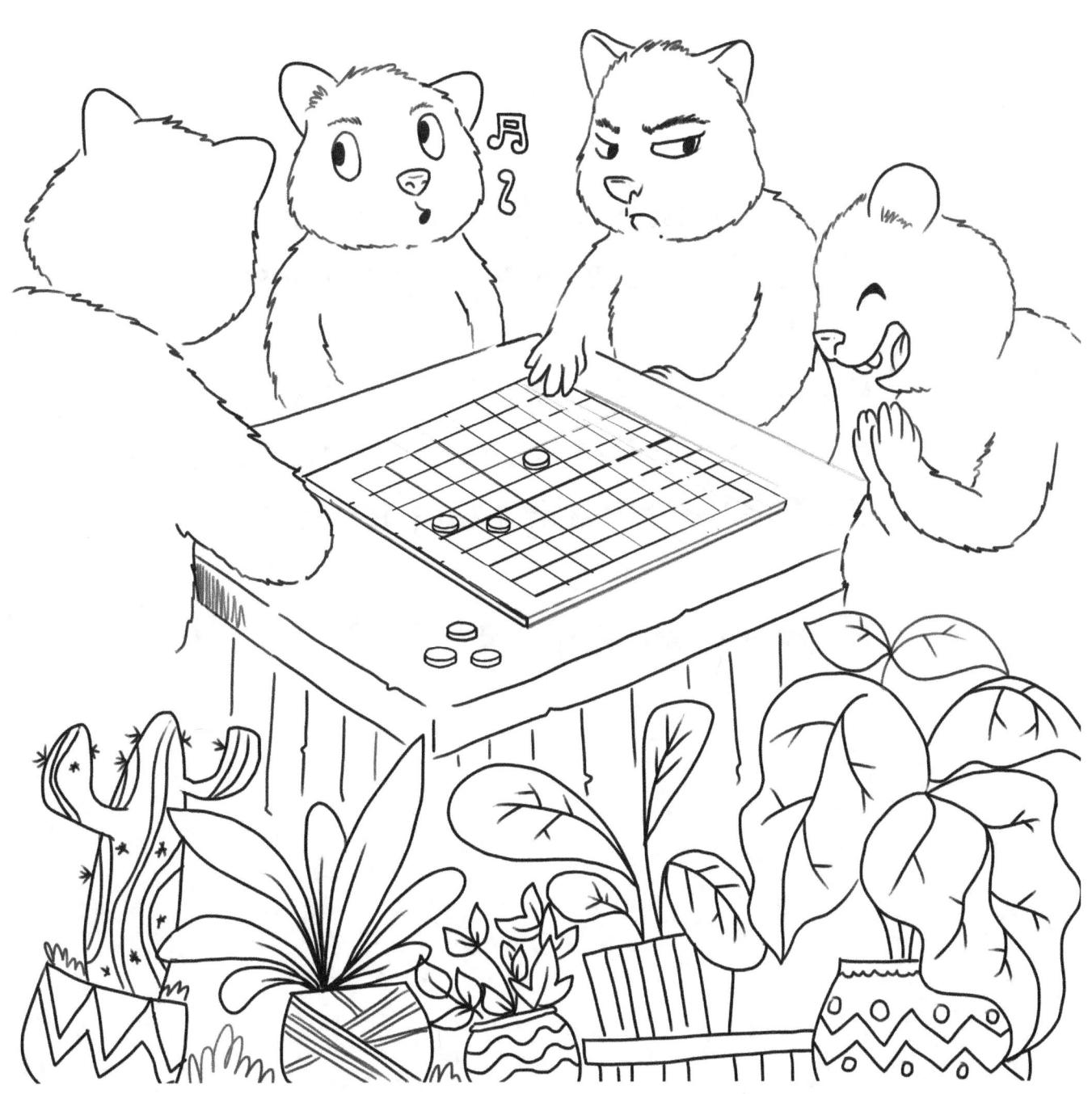

Time for another prime time dating show... *Questionable Quokkas!*

Quokkas are known to choose the same mate multiple years in a row, but they do not necessarily mate for life.

In human terms, they can't commit.

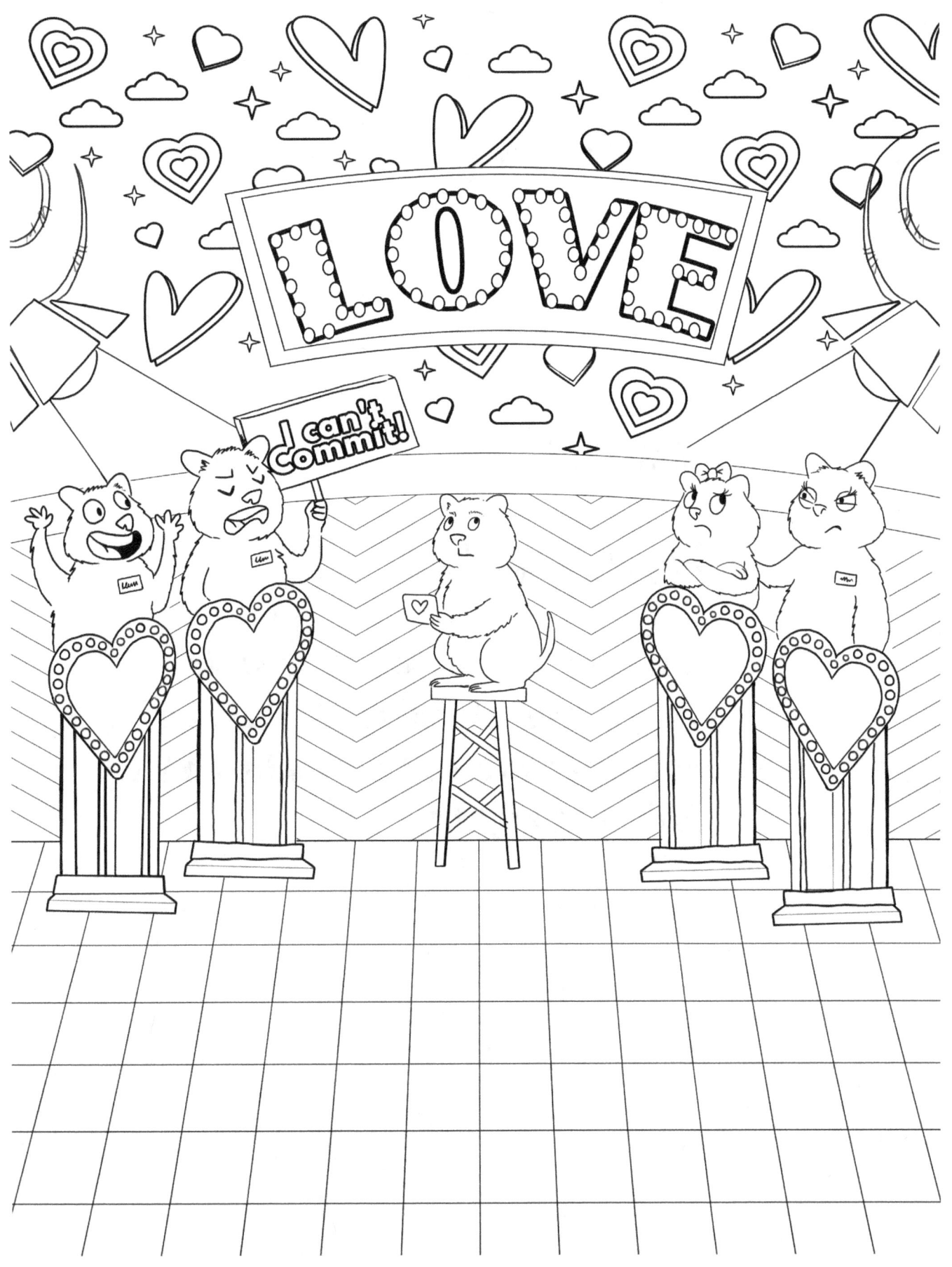

Night owl?

No, night quokka!

Quokkas are nocturnal animals.
They prefer sleeping all day and
doing activities like laundry and
dishes at night.

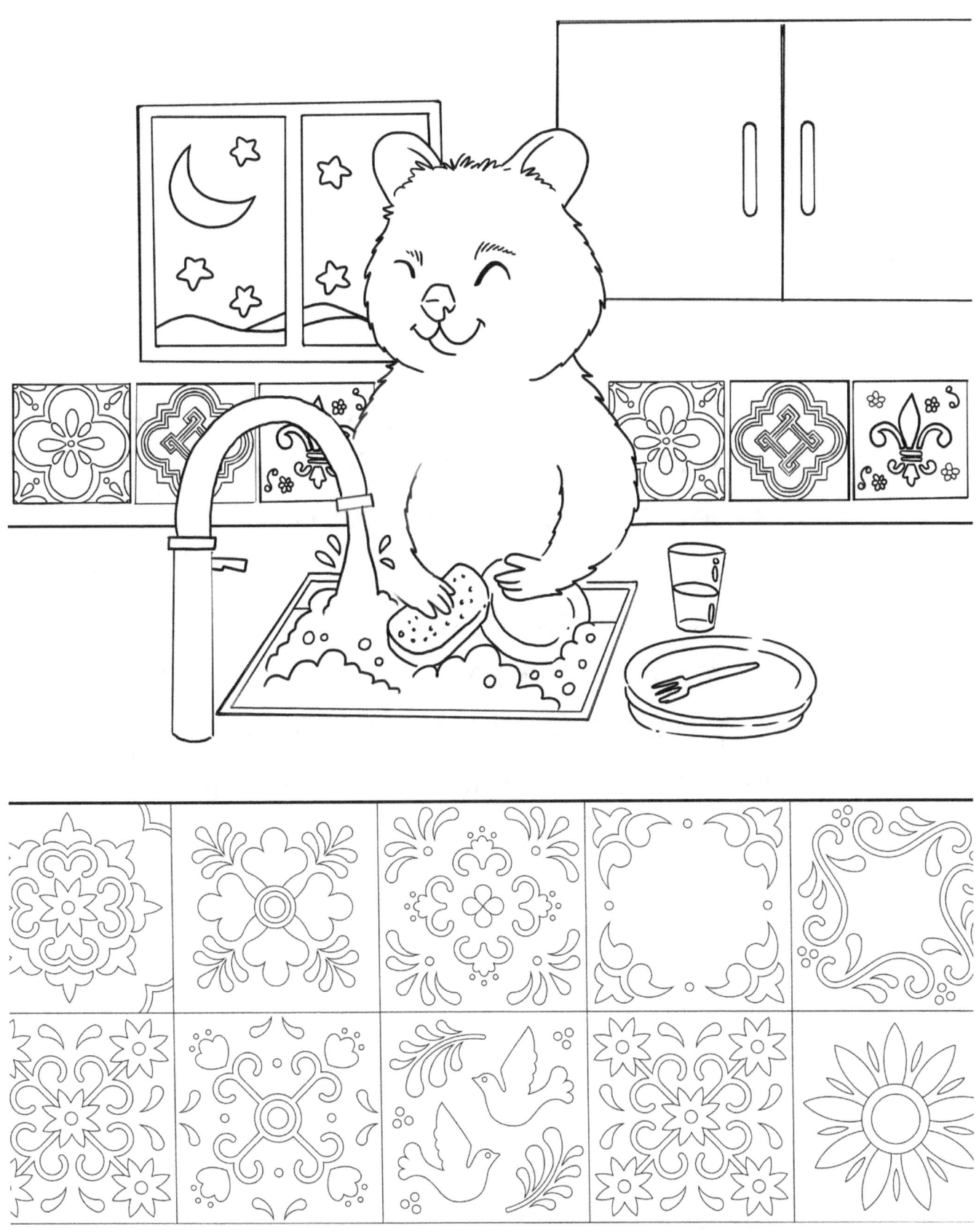

Quokkas are mammals and, like most mammals, they give birth to live young and nurse their joeys.

In spite of their cuteness, we have never ever seen a quokka lay an egg, not even on holidays where other mammals are reported to lay eggs.

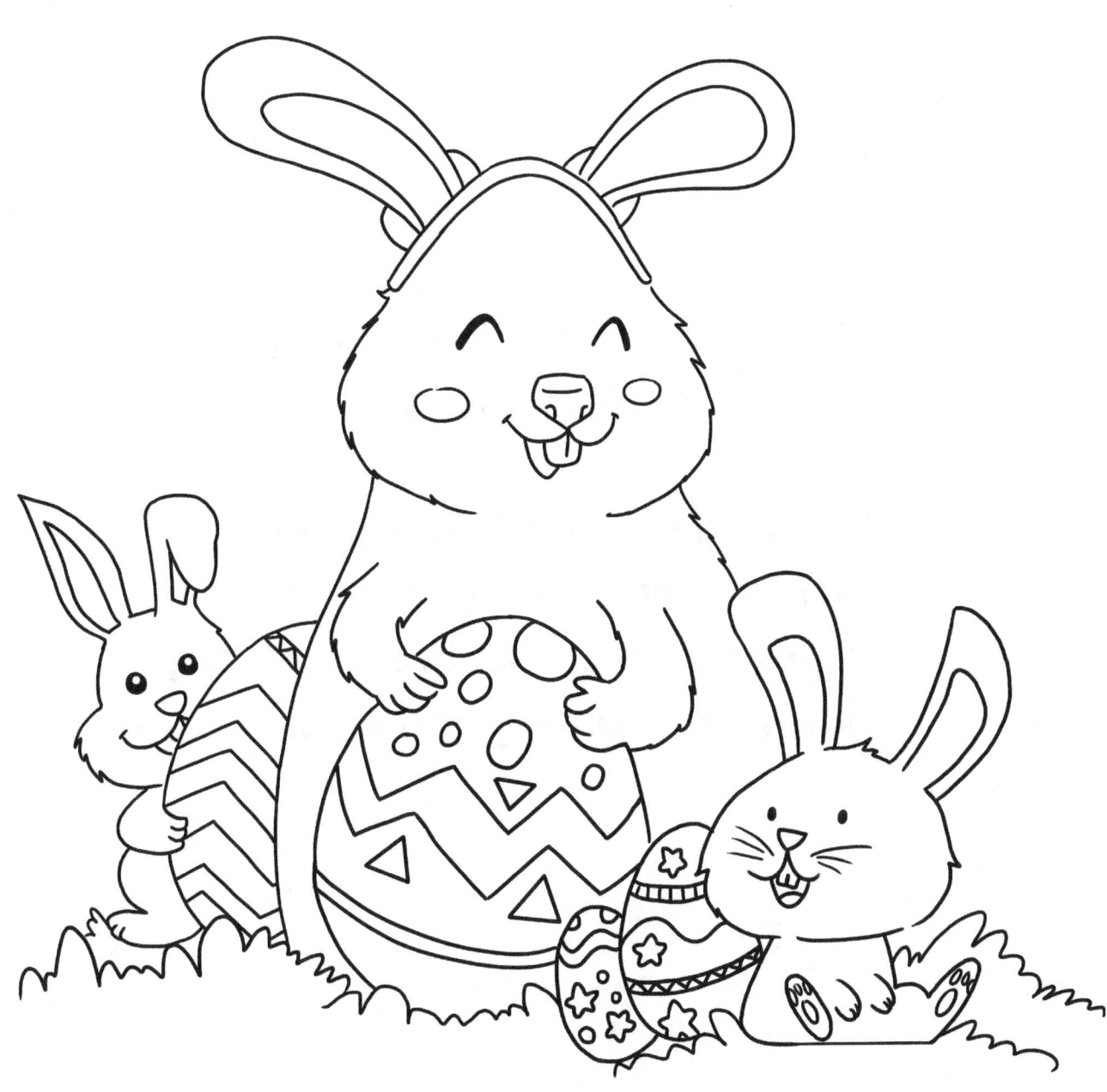

There is no official quokka mating season on the mainland.

On Rottnest and Bald Islands, quokkas breed only once per year and joeys are born in springtime, between February and April.

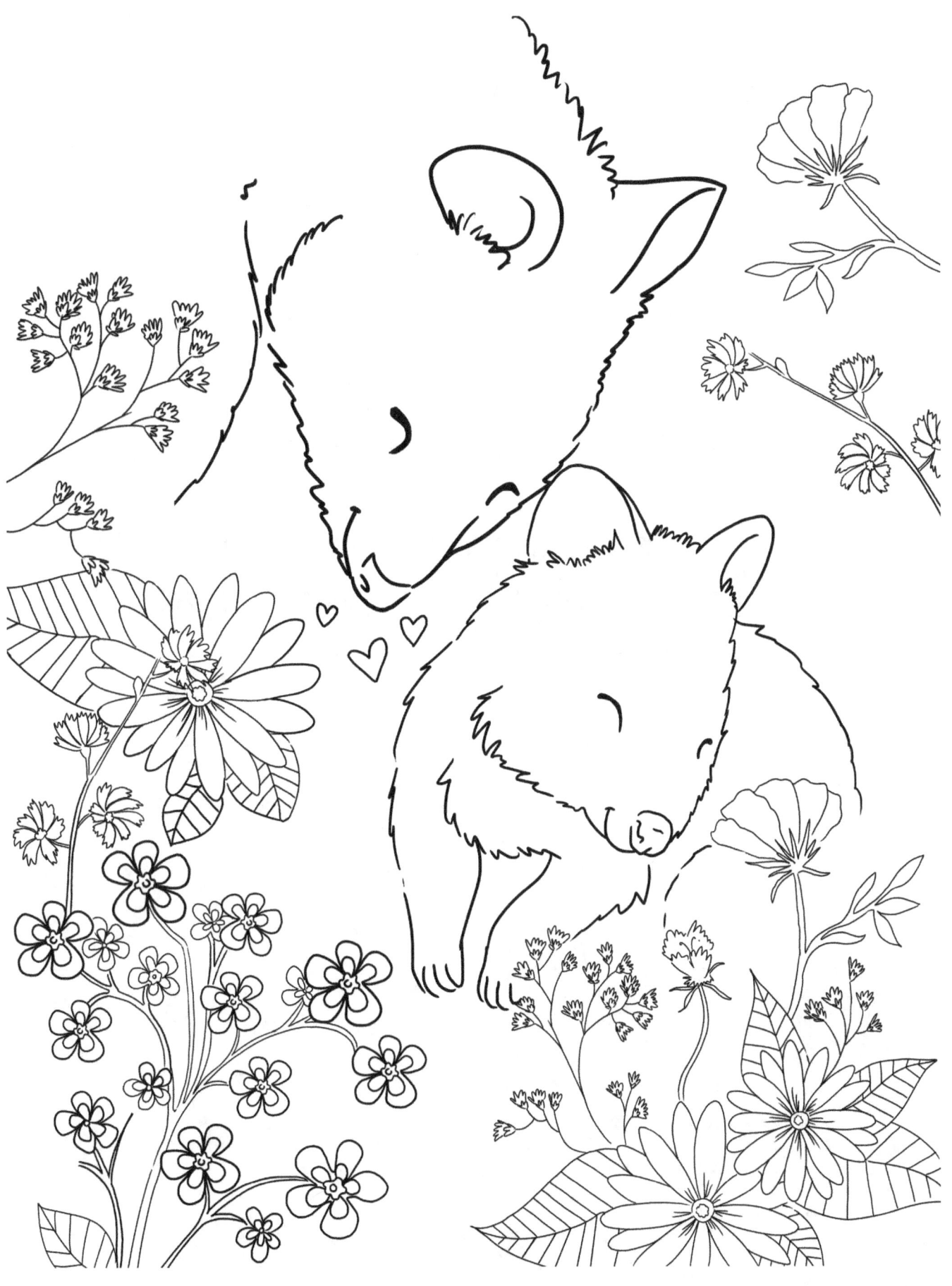

Quokkas can reproduce quite quickly.

A female can have up to 2 babies per year and up to 17 babies in her lifetime.

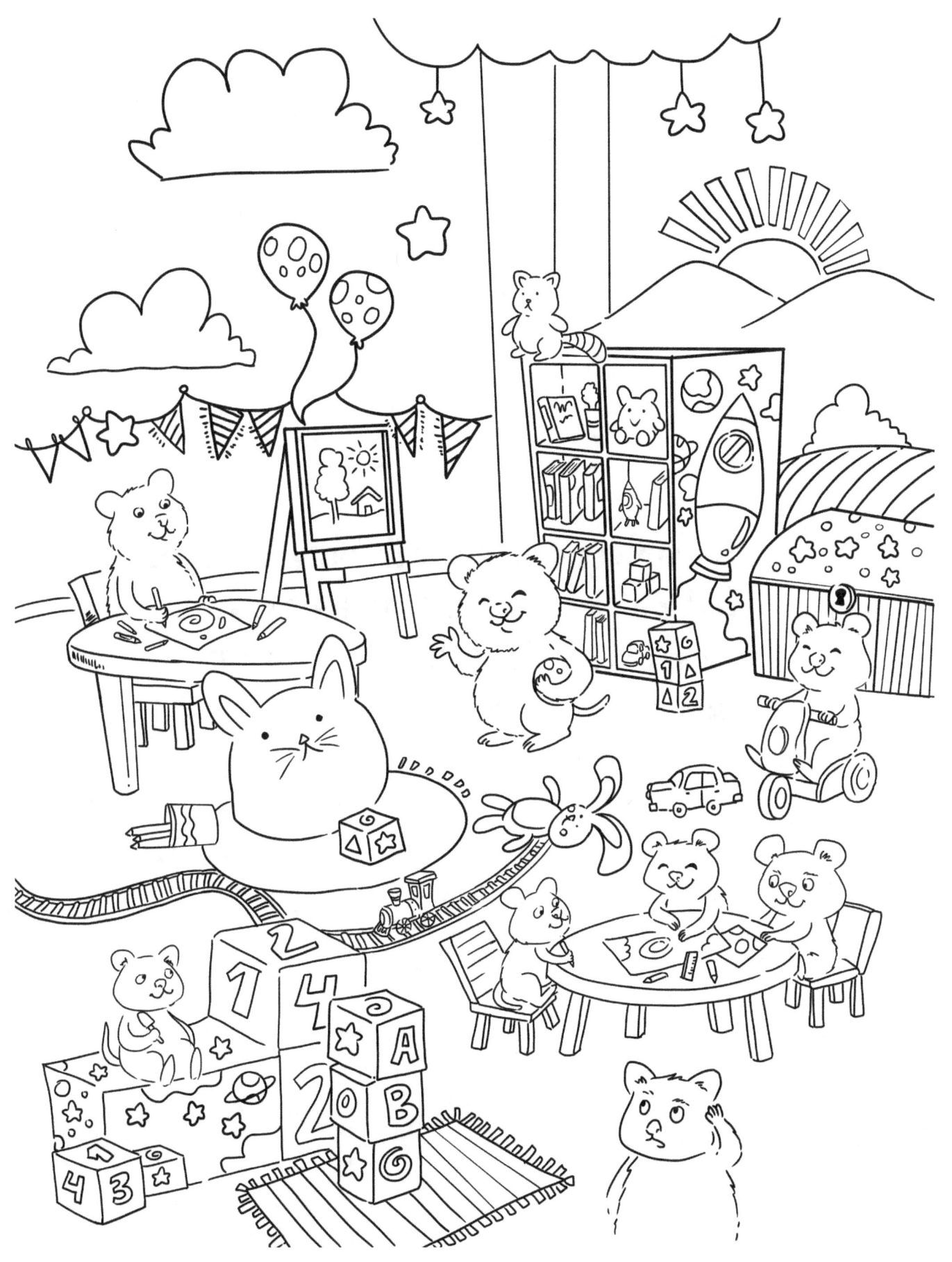

A mamma quokka will only have one baby at a time, and often nurse and care for her joey for the first six months of its life.

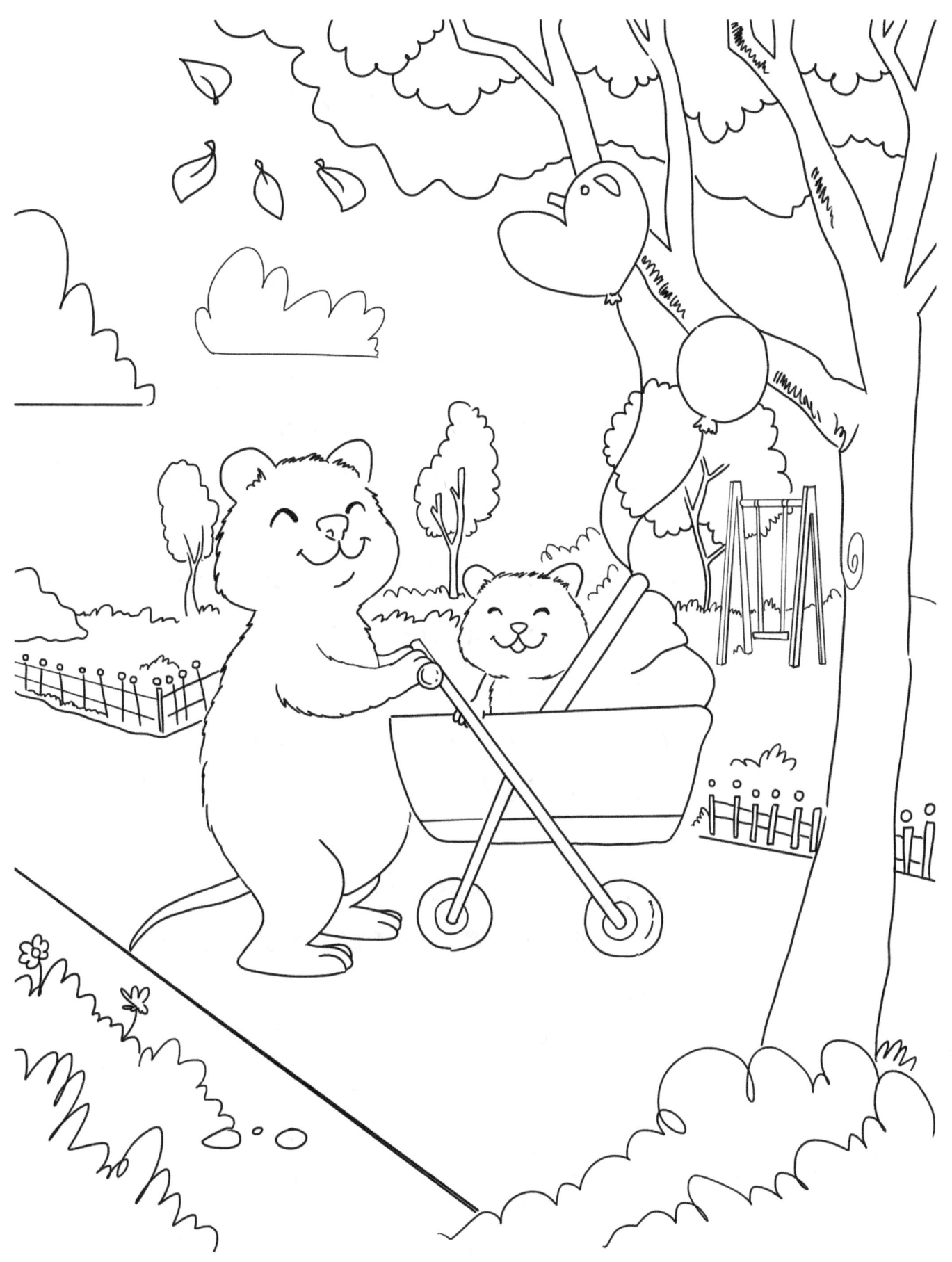

At six months old, a joey will begin to eat whole foods and learn to fend for itself.

By the end of the first year, the joey is considered an independent adult and doesn't need his mom's permission to stay out late!

Can you imagine if human one-year-olds were considered adults?

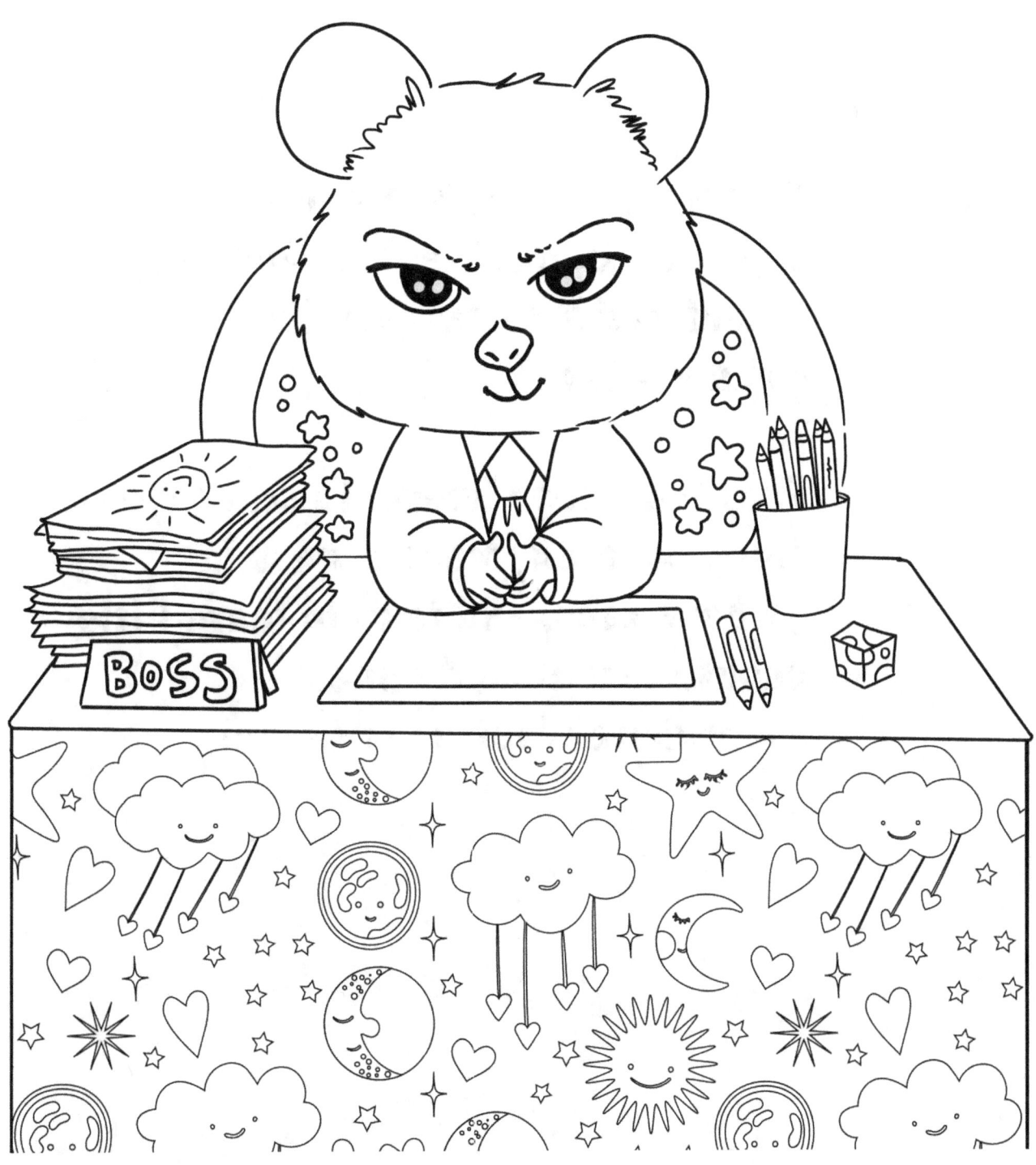

Despite their very charming appearance, quokkas are sometimes considered a nuisance in local communities.

They have been known to scavenge and steal food, make a mess in garbage cans, and tend to leave little quokka-sized 'land mines' everywhere. Watch your step!

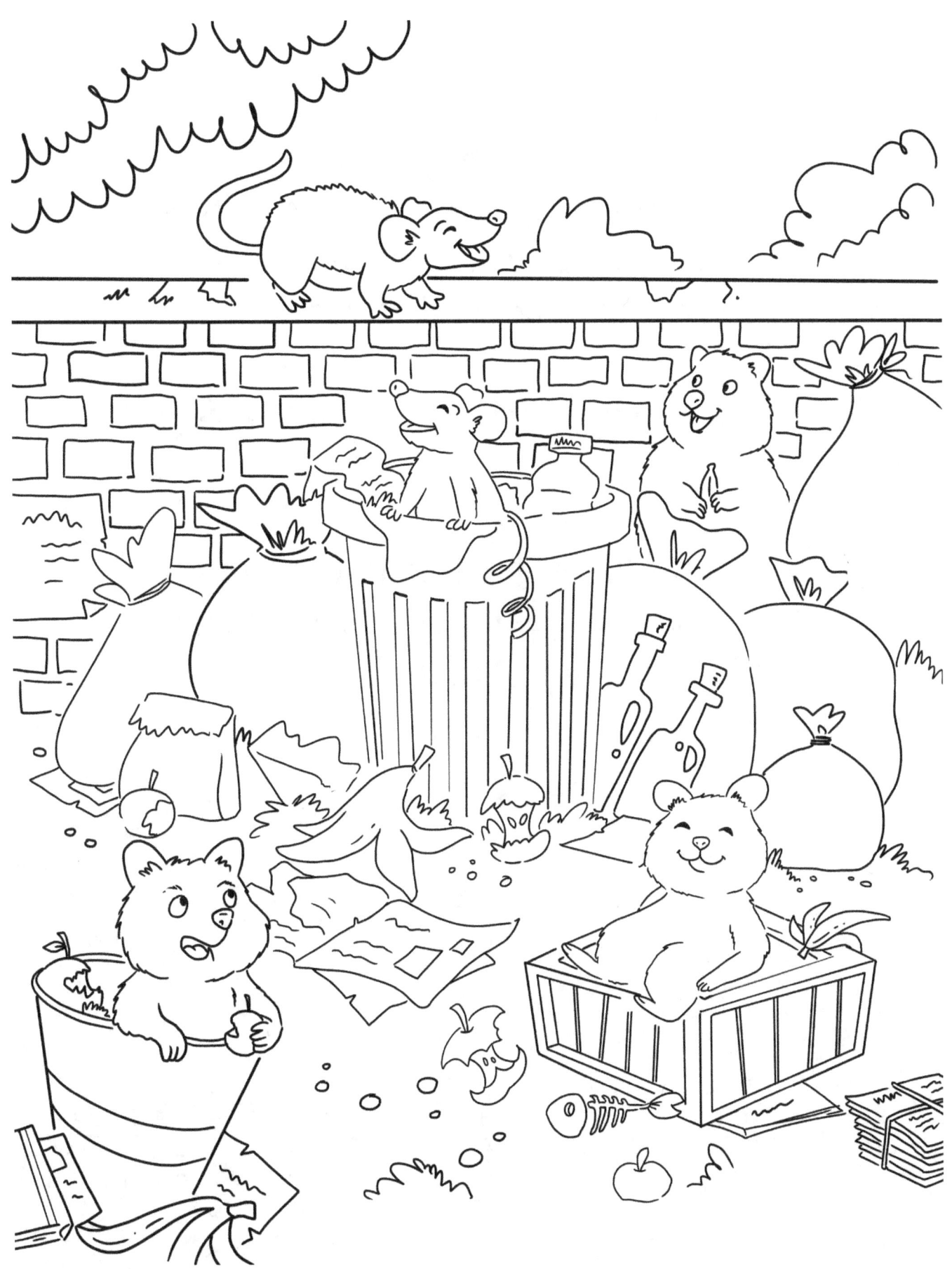

Quokkas spend much of their lives in riparian habitats. These are areas of lush vegetation along rivers and streams.

Capybara friends...how'd you get here?

We know you like rivers and streams, but how'd you get all the way to Australia?

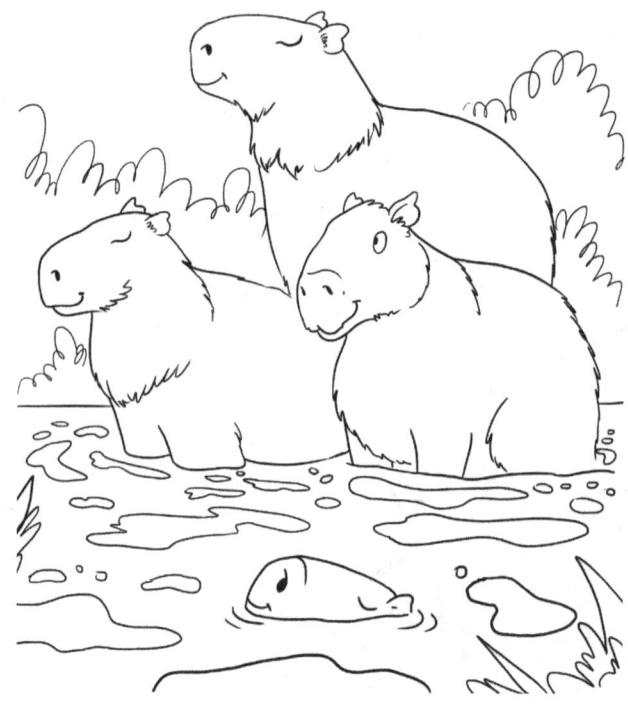

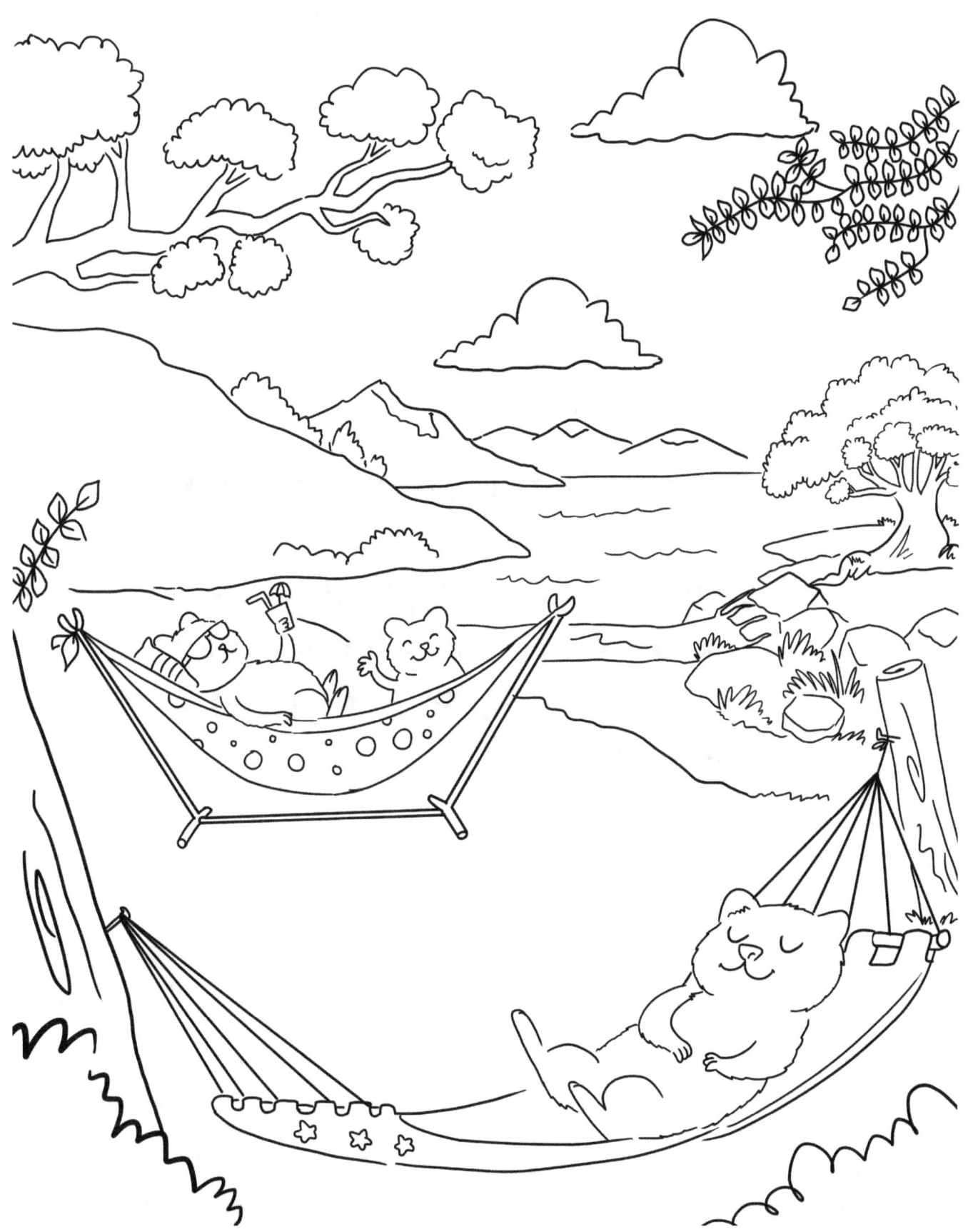

Quokkas move around quite a bit.

Their territory ranges from small areas to vast expanses depending on rainfall levels, food availability, and location.

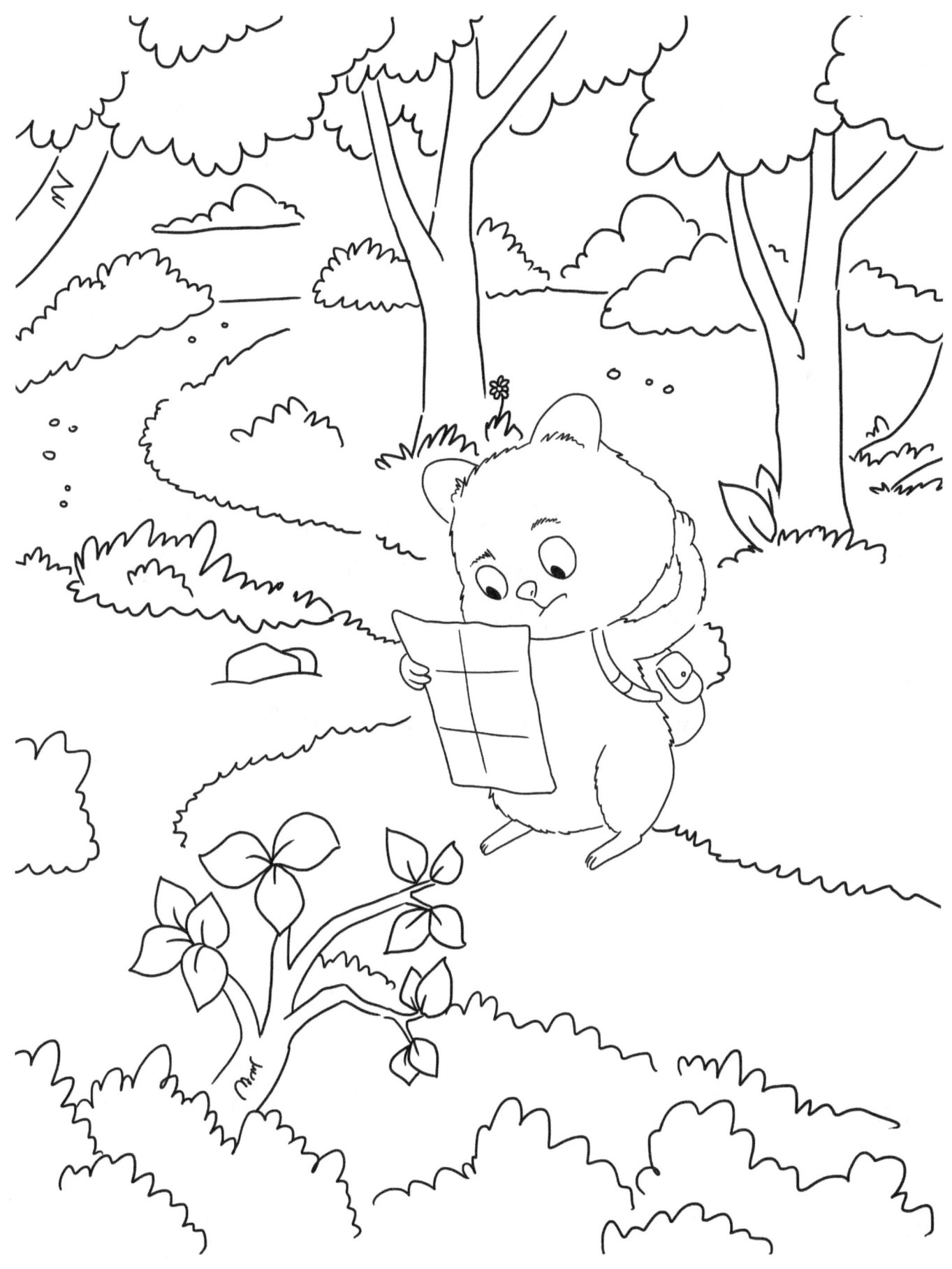

Would you like to see a quokka? If you do, you'll have to plan a vacation to Australia or the zoo.

One rule: please invite me!

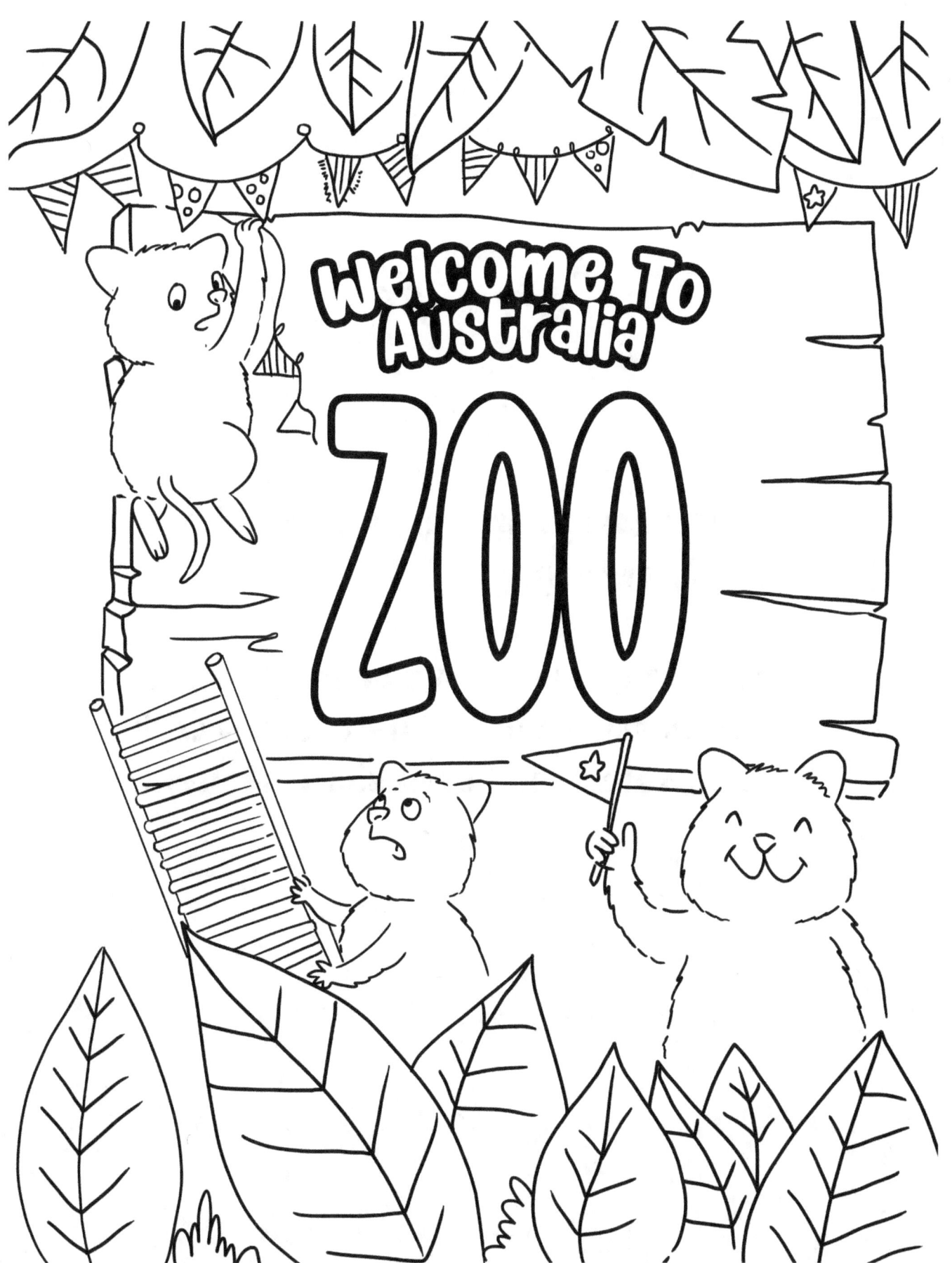

Male quokkas are very territorial and rarely overlap.

Female quokkas have been known to live in small groups, particularly with their young, and even share shelters.

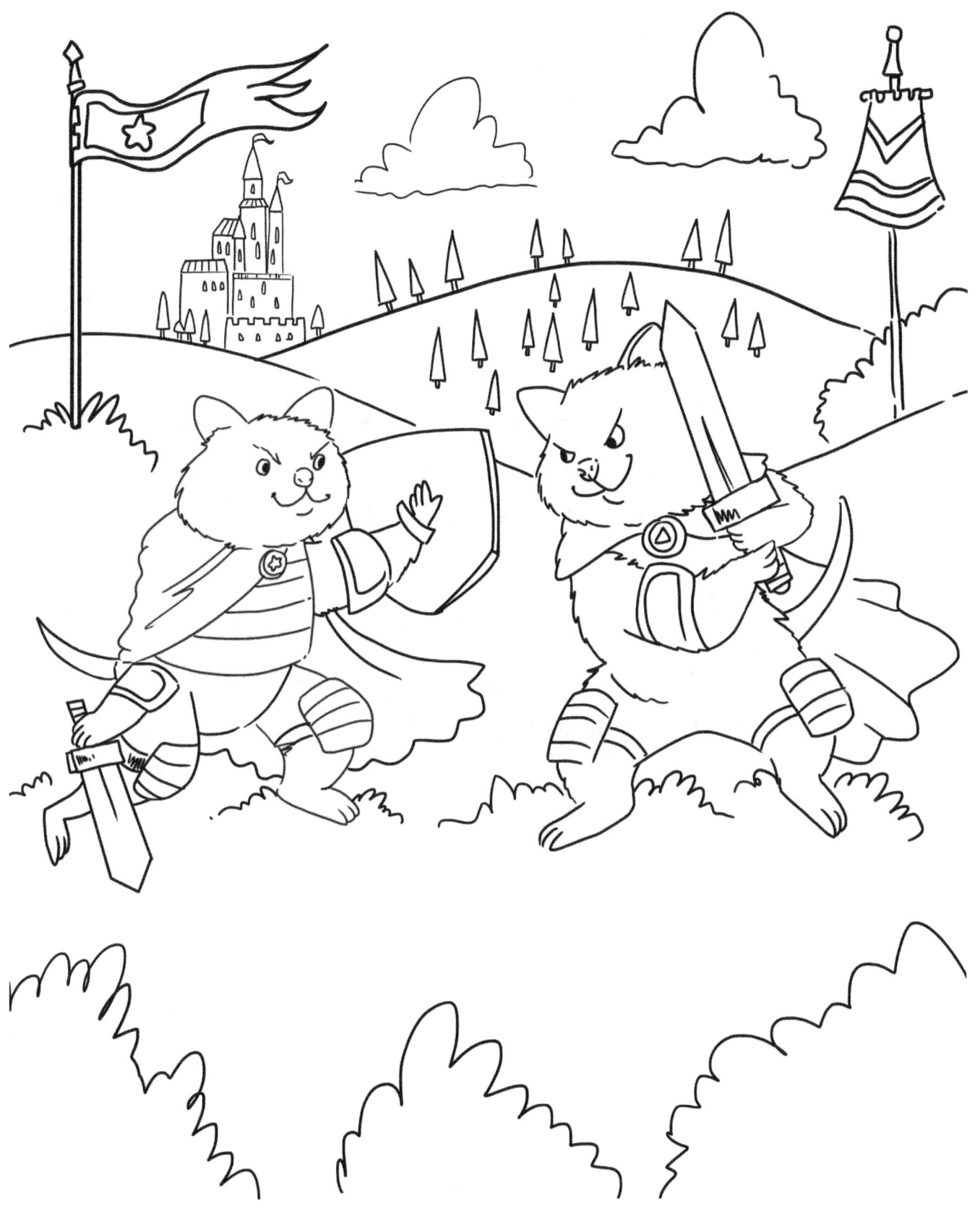

Some researchers have found that quokkas on Rottnest Island are more committed to their relationships.

They believe that some engage in monogamous mating pairs for several years at a time.

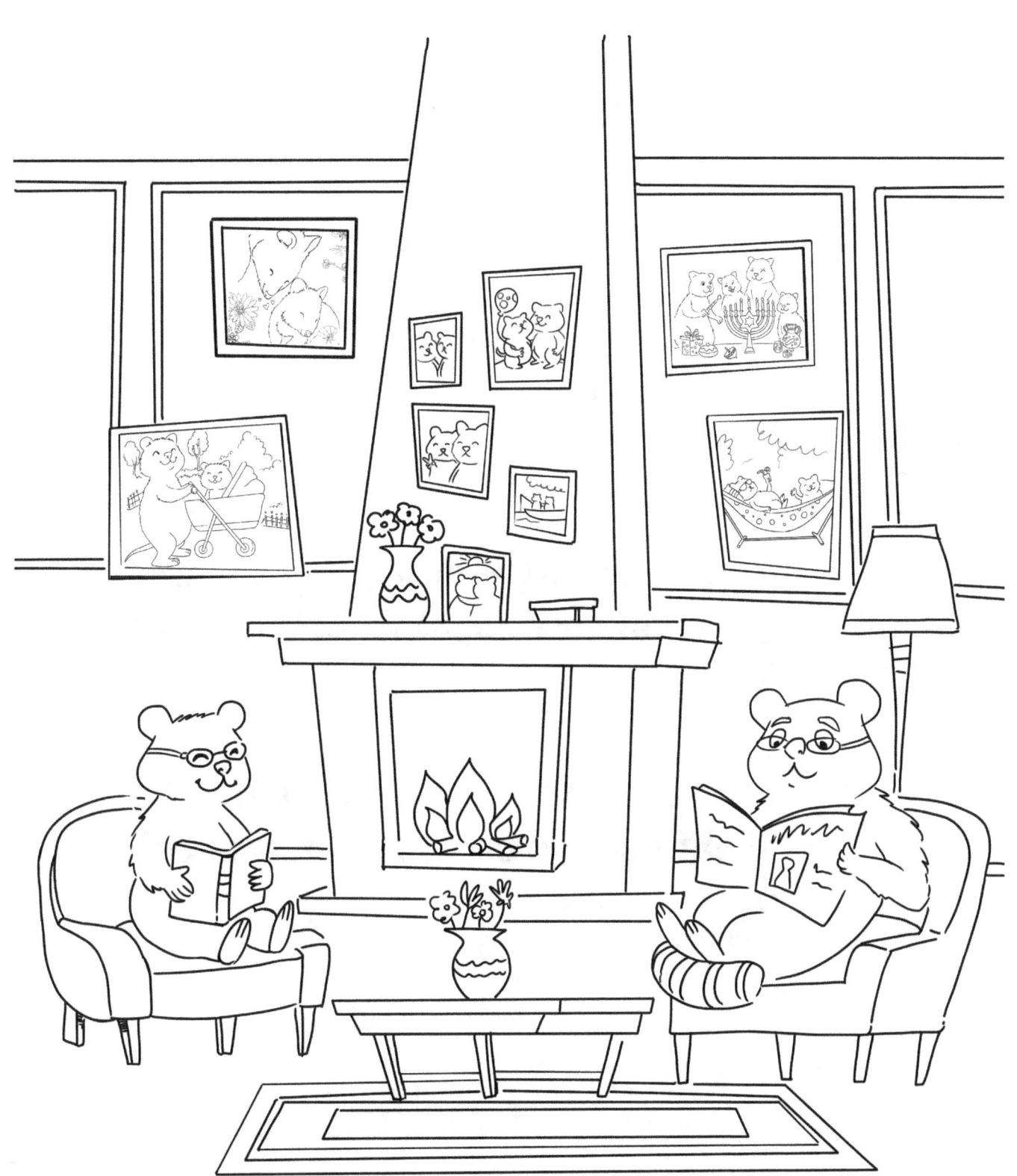

Despite having four legs, quokkas get around by hopping on their back legs.

They can also crawl on all fours. You might say quokkas have four-wheel-drive.

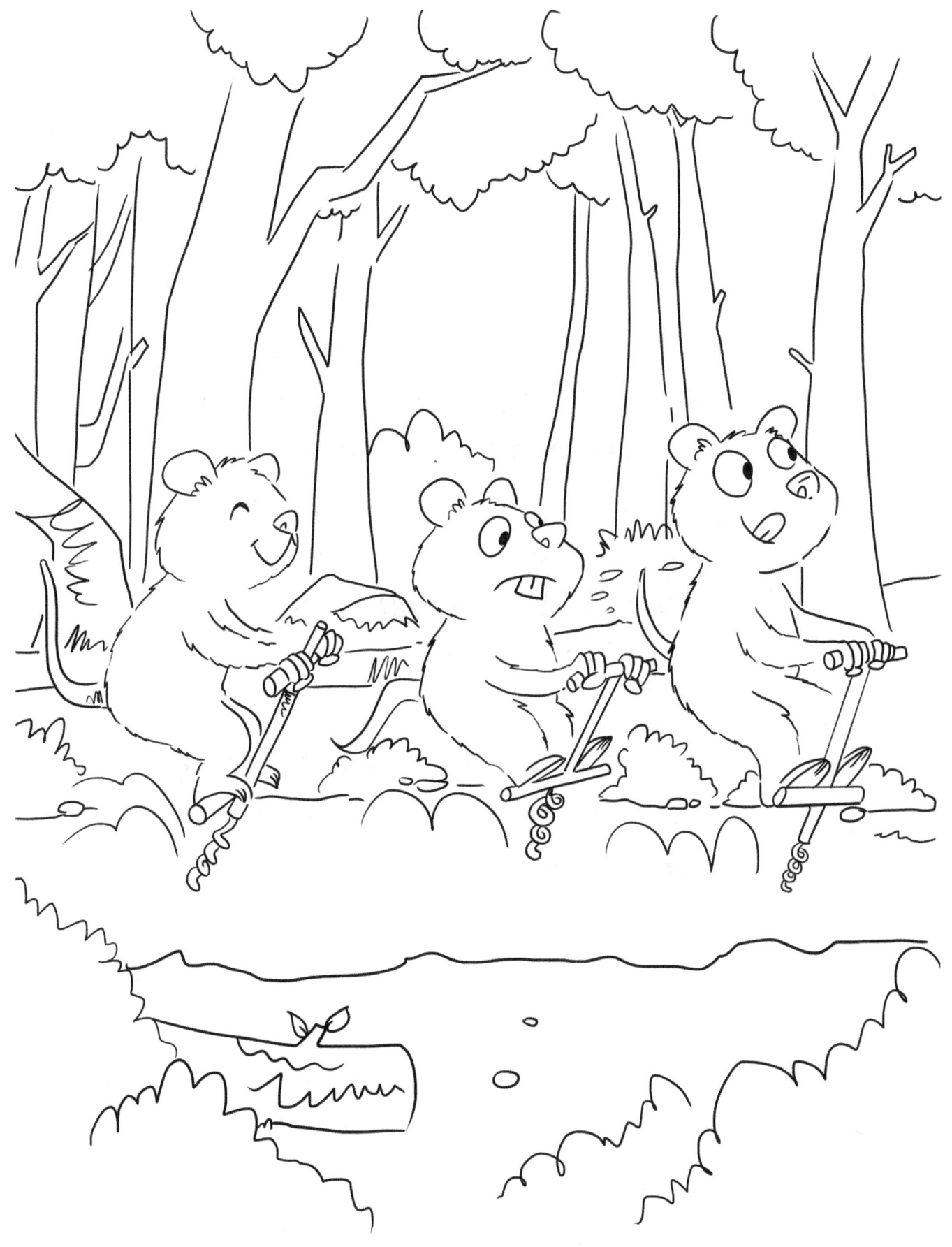

Did you know quokkas can climb trees? They normally hang out on the ground, but they can climb heights of up to six feet!

After that, they get a bit scared of heights.

Please make sure to maintain a safe distance from the ground while coloring.

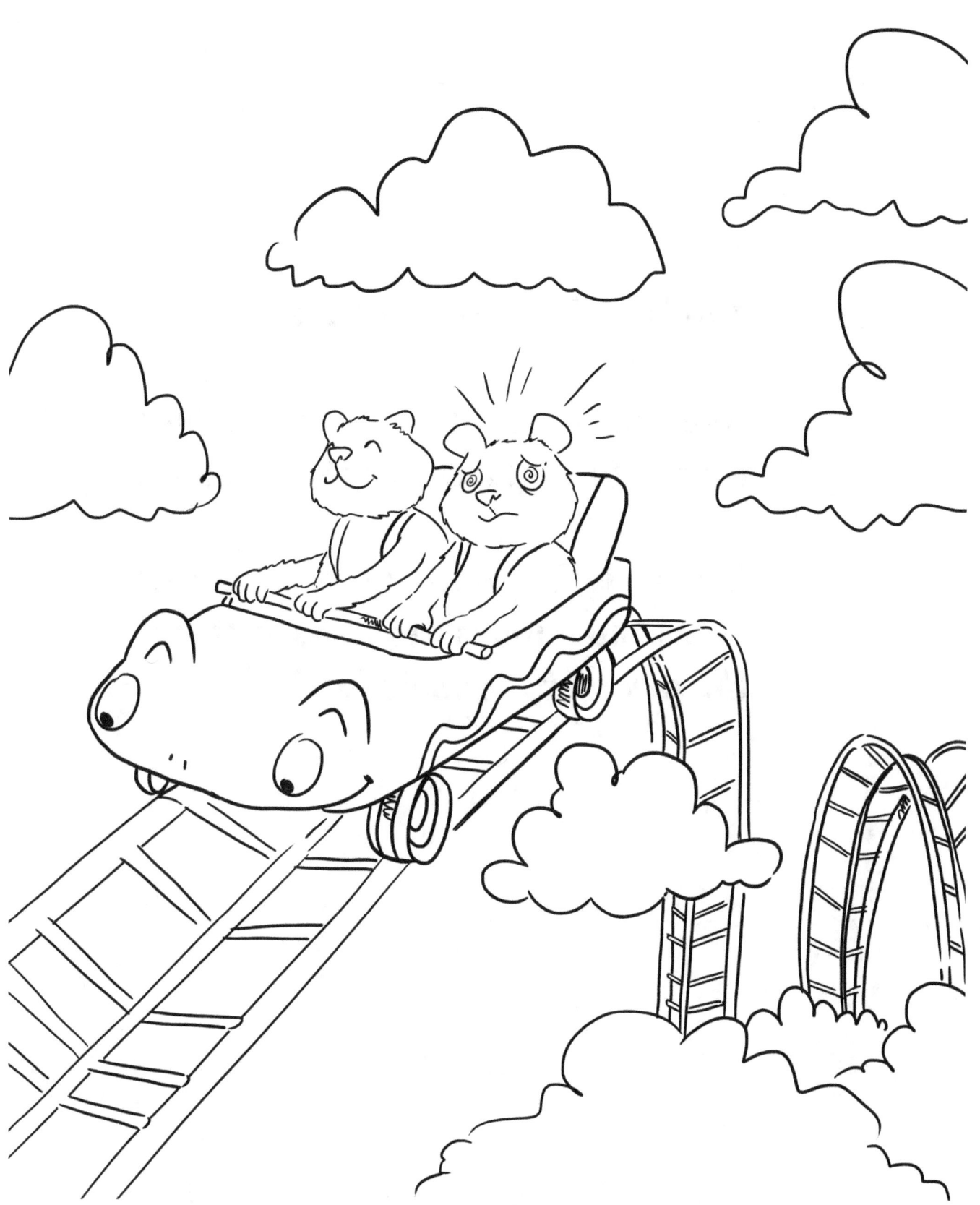

You'll find no table manners here.

Quokkas often eat their food whole, then throw up and eat the leftovers!

Gross, right? Actually, this process helps the quokkas to absorb all of the nutrients in their food.

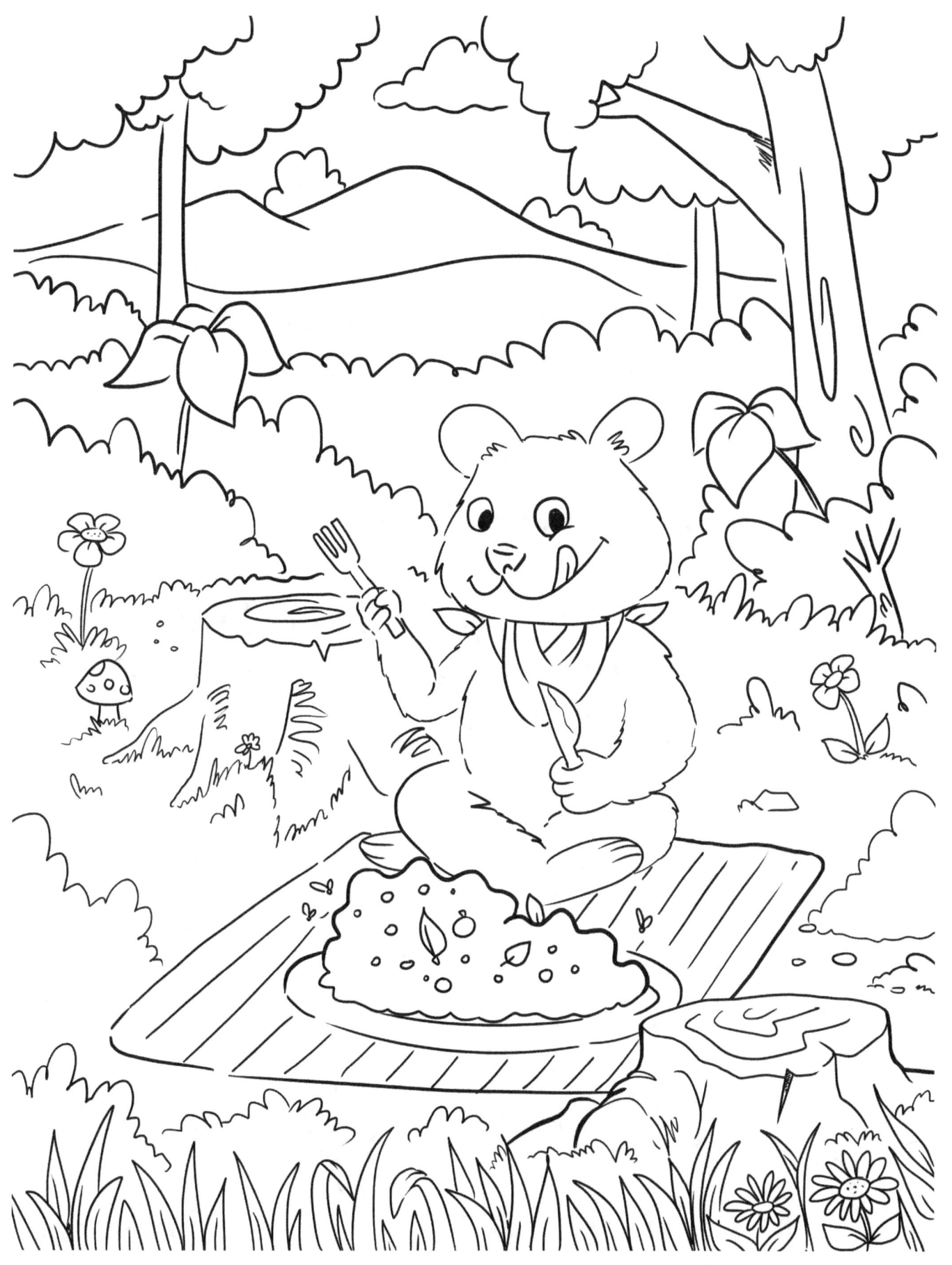

Quokkas are usually peaceful creatures, unlike their kangaroo cousins.

Quokkas typically only fight when threatened or in danger.

But be careful, quokkas have long, sharp teeth and claws they will use if you get too close!

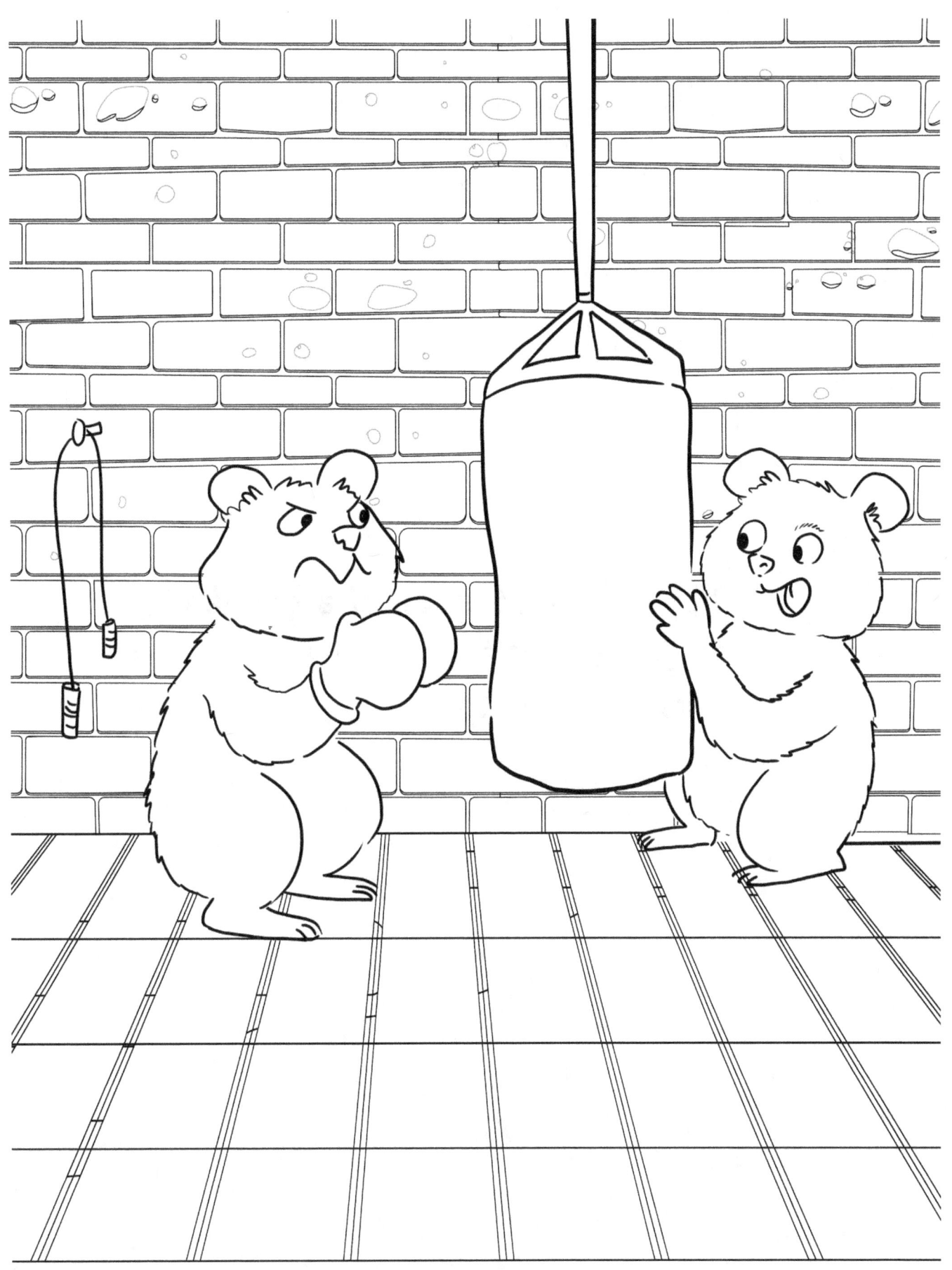

The average lifespan of a quokka is ten years, but they can live up to 14 years in captivity.

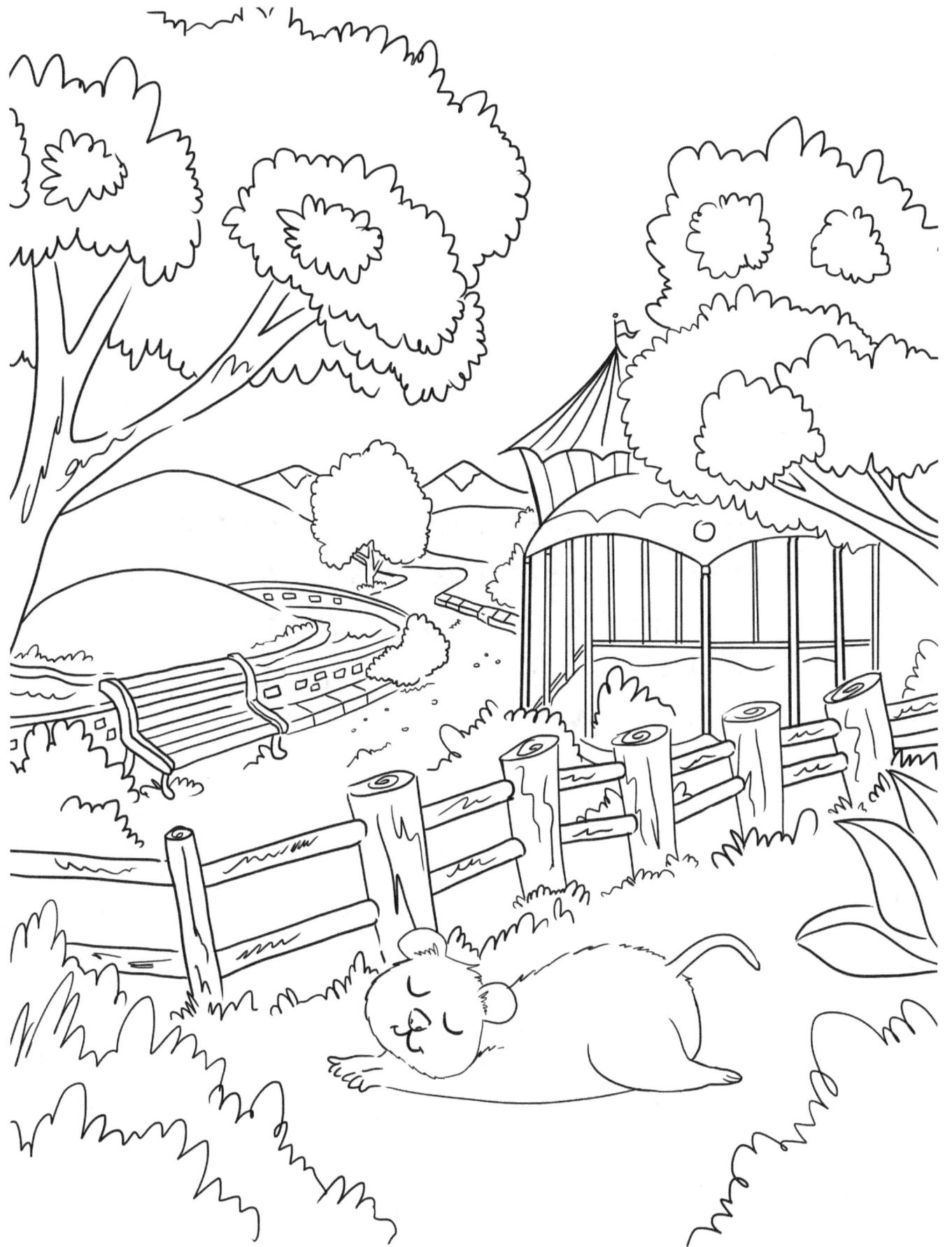

Quokkas love people-watching! No, really! On Rottnest Island the quokkas' favorite pastime is watching the visitors (and stealing your snacks).

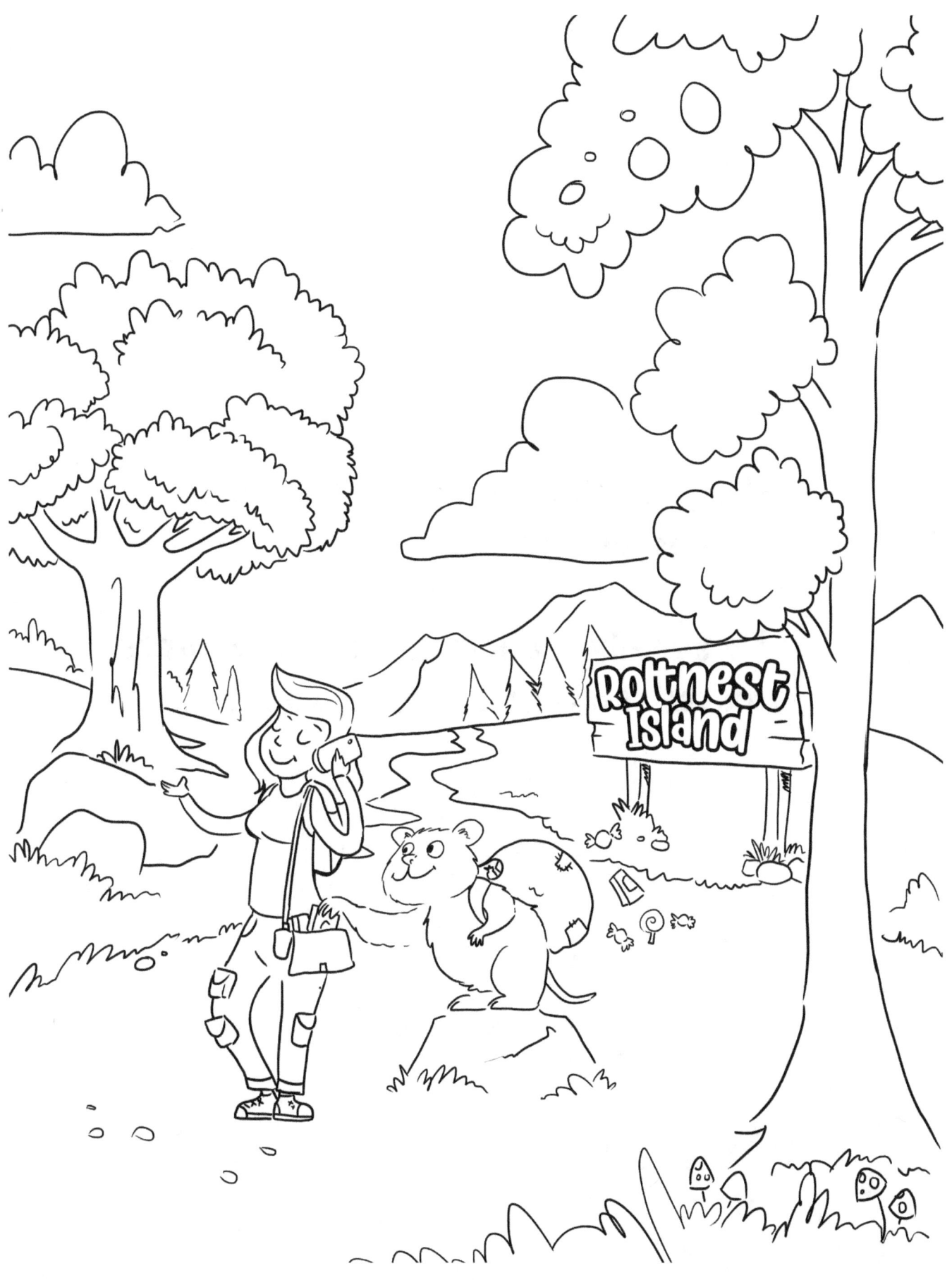

Many famous celebrities have taken photos with quokkas.

Personally, I'd like to see more quokkas on the red carpet in Hollywood!

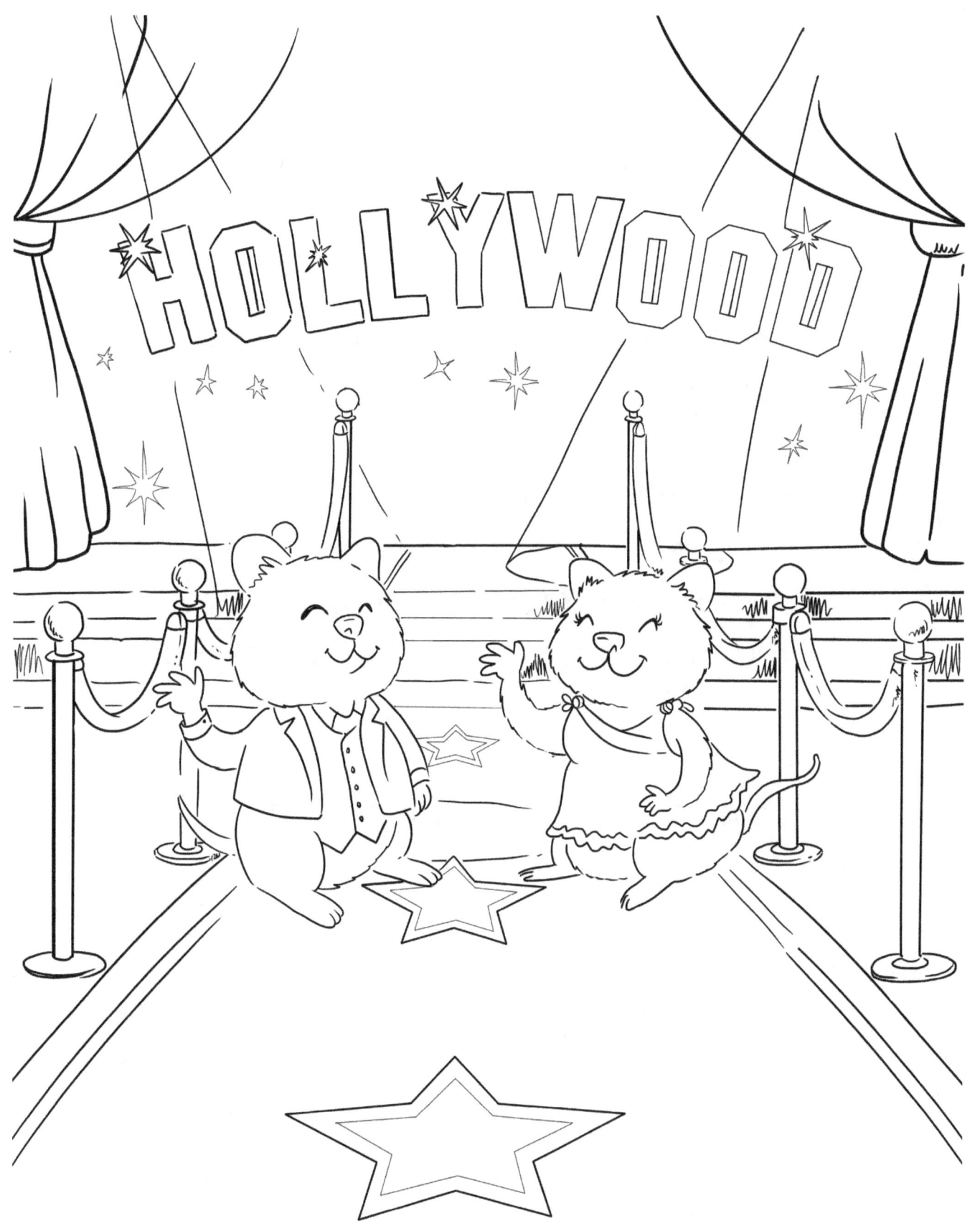

Want to help save the quokka? Try eating one!

Not really, of course. Try the chocolate version. Some candy stores on Rottnest Island make miniature chocolate quokkas to raise money for environmental conservation.

Tasty and good for the planet!

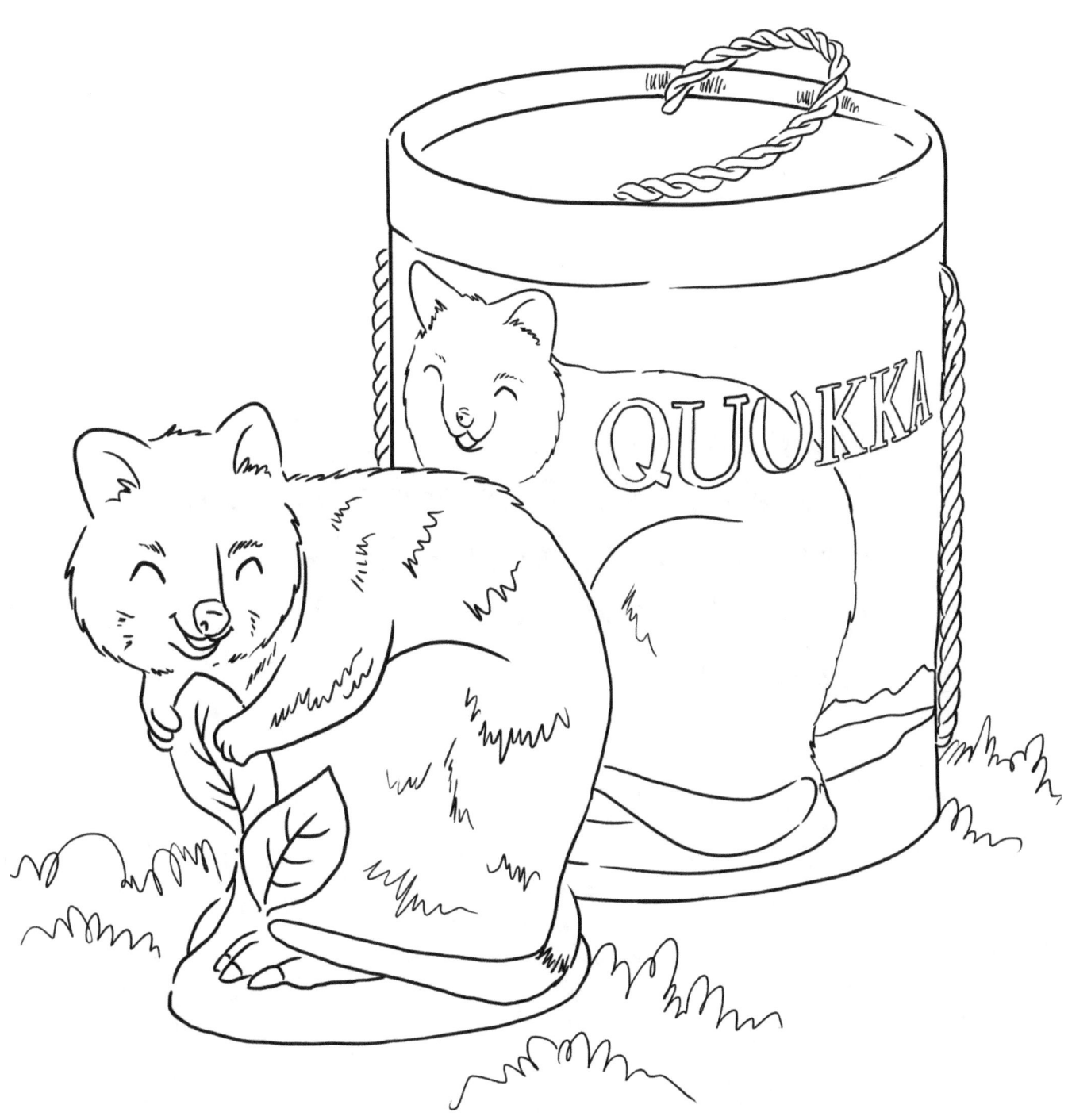

The quokka is a survivor. By climbing to find food and developing clever ways of storing fat, the quokka has proven very resilient and resourceful.

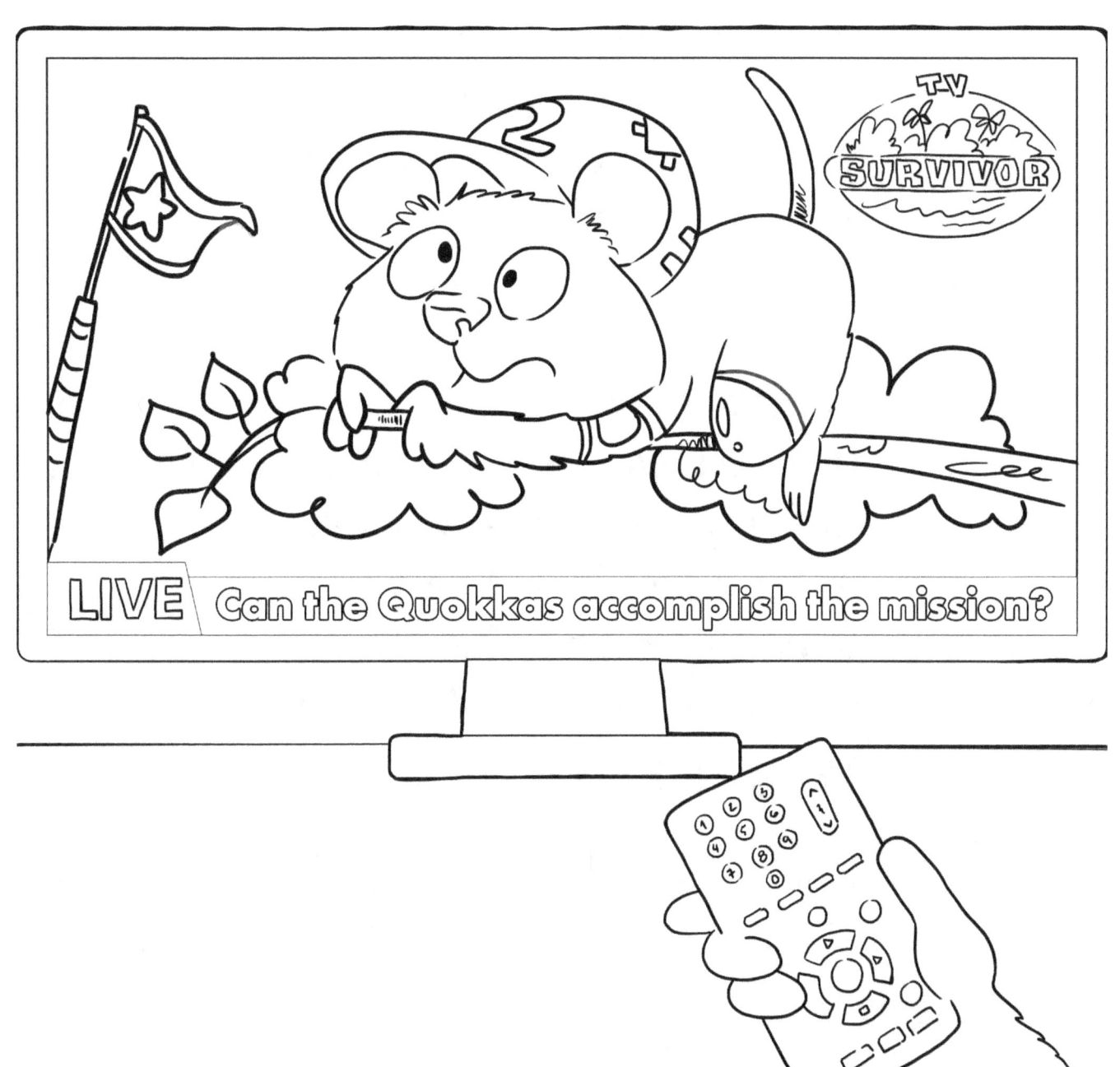

Thirsty? The quokka isn't! When water is scarce, quokkas have even been known to chow down on succulent plants for hydration.

Packing on the pounds (or kilograms for our international readers)! Much like a camel stores water in its humps, quokkas can store fat in their tails to access when food and water are scarce.

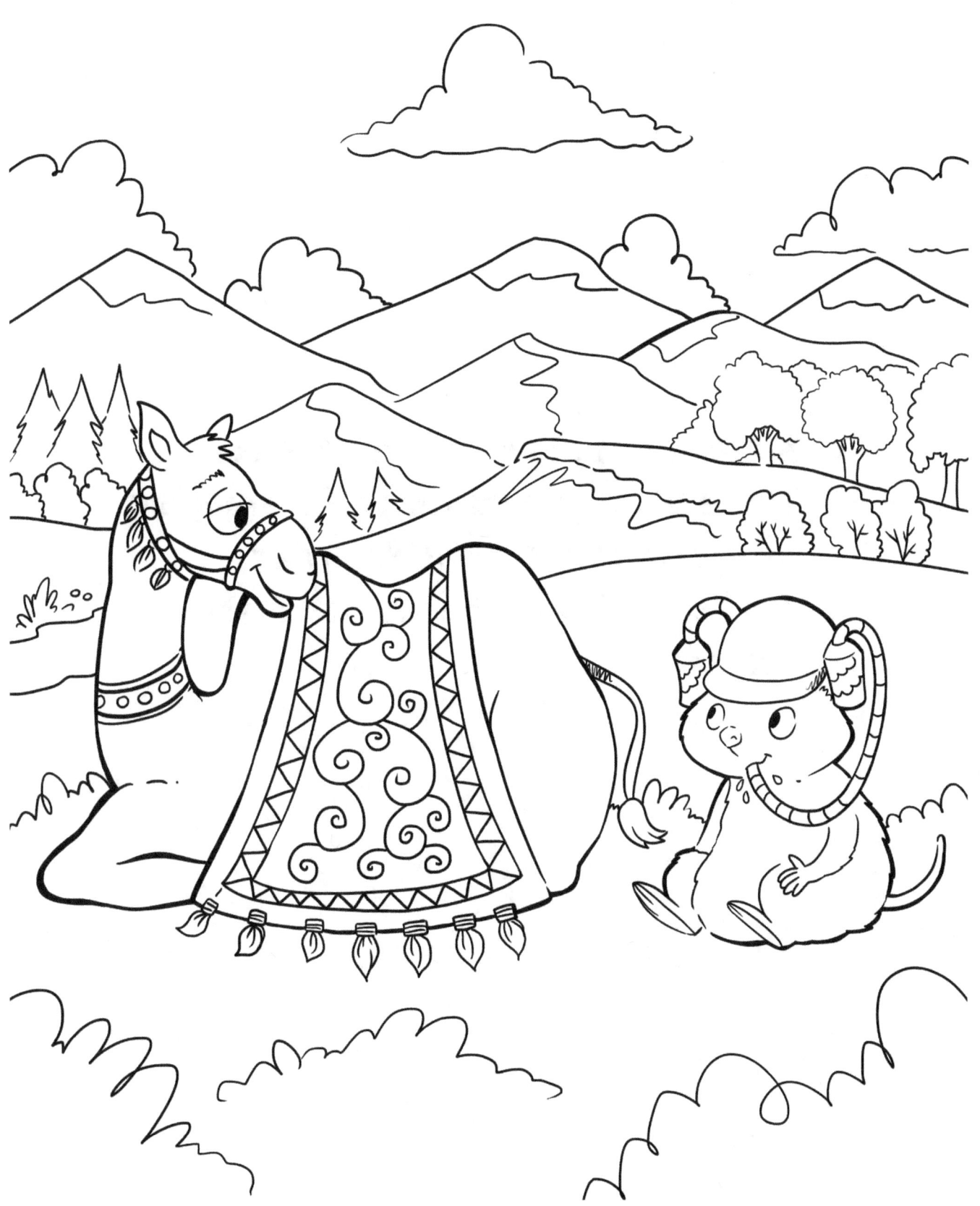

No feather pillows for the quokka. These little guys much prefer sleeping in a plant called *Acanthocarpus preissii* and take shelter under the spiky fronds.

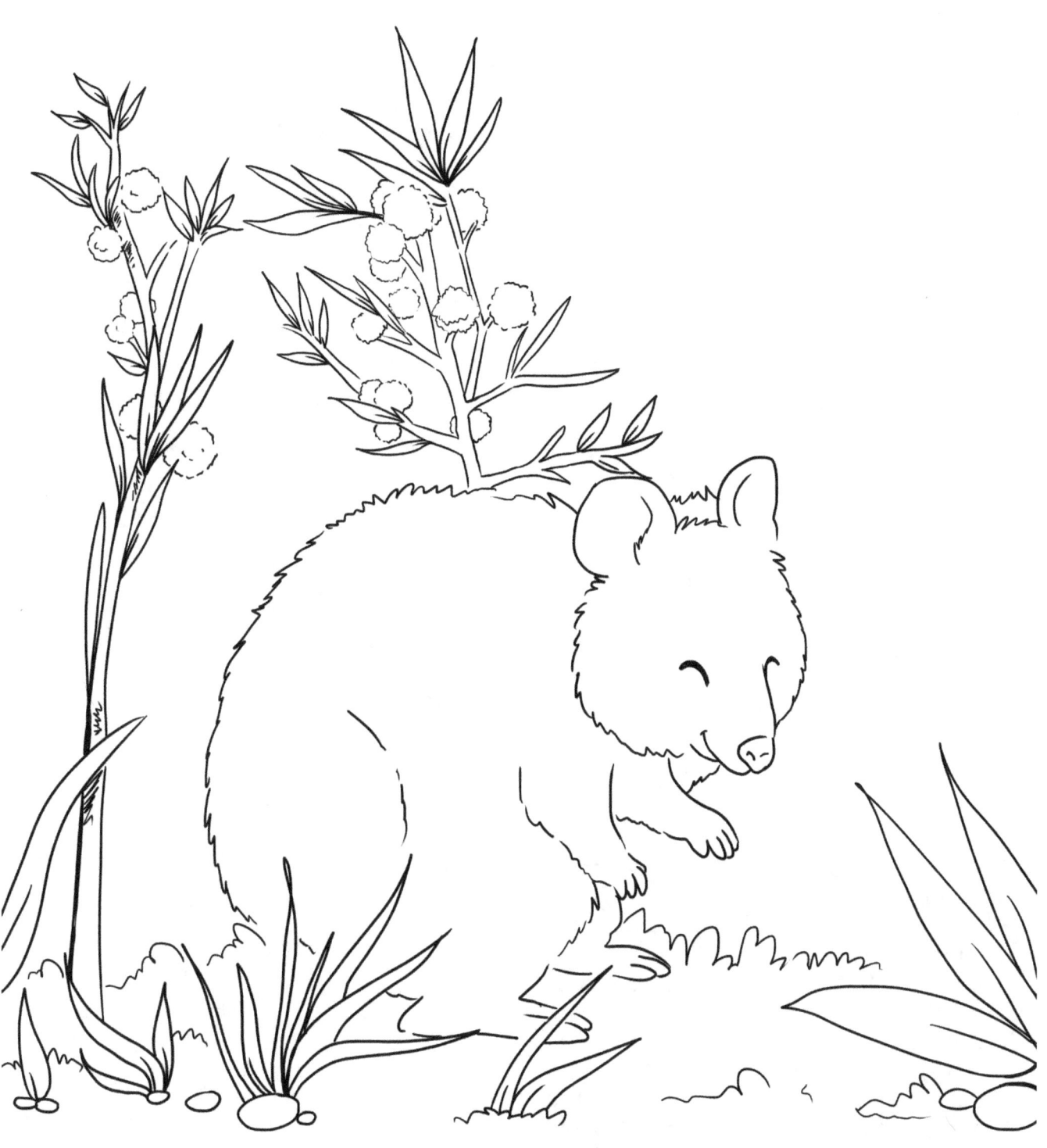

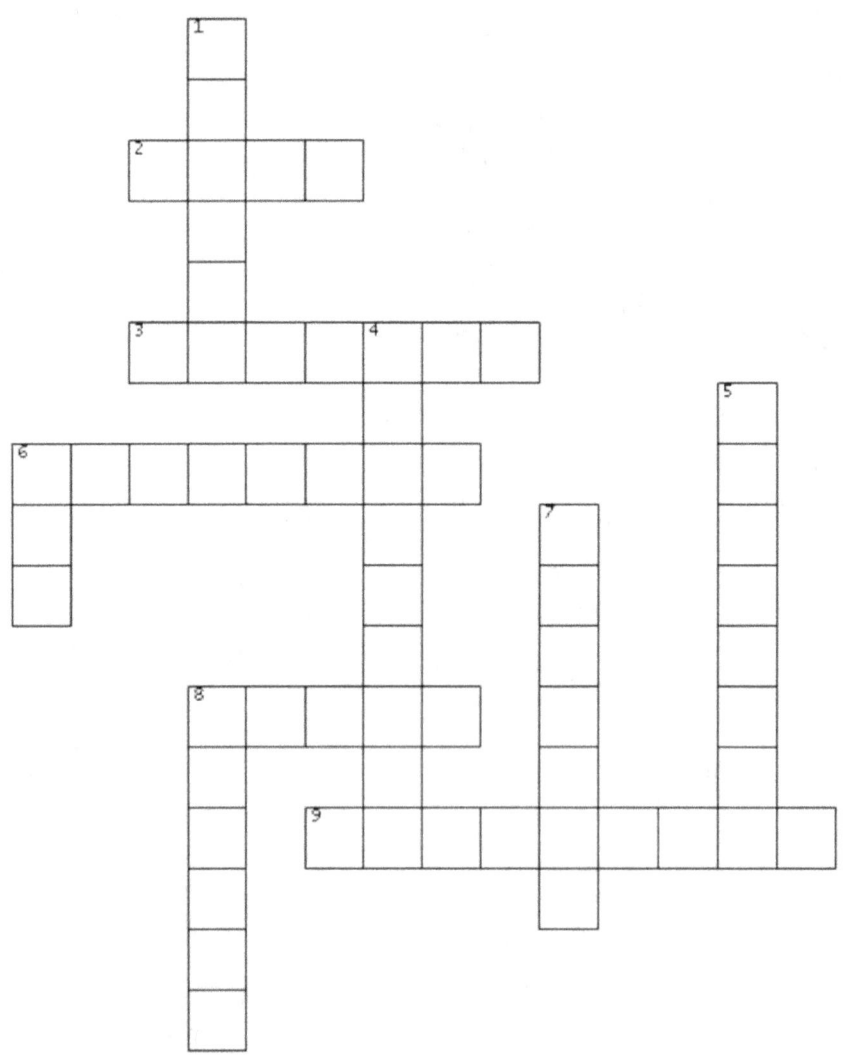

ACROSS
2. a baby quokka (note: also a character from *Friends*)
3. the quokka is a small version of this animal
6. the island where quokkas are commonly found
8. a toothy grin
9. the scientific family quokka belongs to

DOWN
1. a very questionable creature
4. the country where our quokka friends live
5. our favorite majestic OG water pig rodent
6. ___, White, and Panda? (hint: a past coloring book pal and animal named "___ Panda")
7. Impossibly...? (hint: a marsupial family member of the quokka and commonly misunderstood animal with a hairless tail)
8. the kind of photo that makes the quokka famous

Use the clues to fill in the words above.

Words can go across or down.
Letters are shared when the words intersect.

How about a word search?

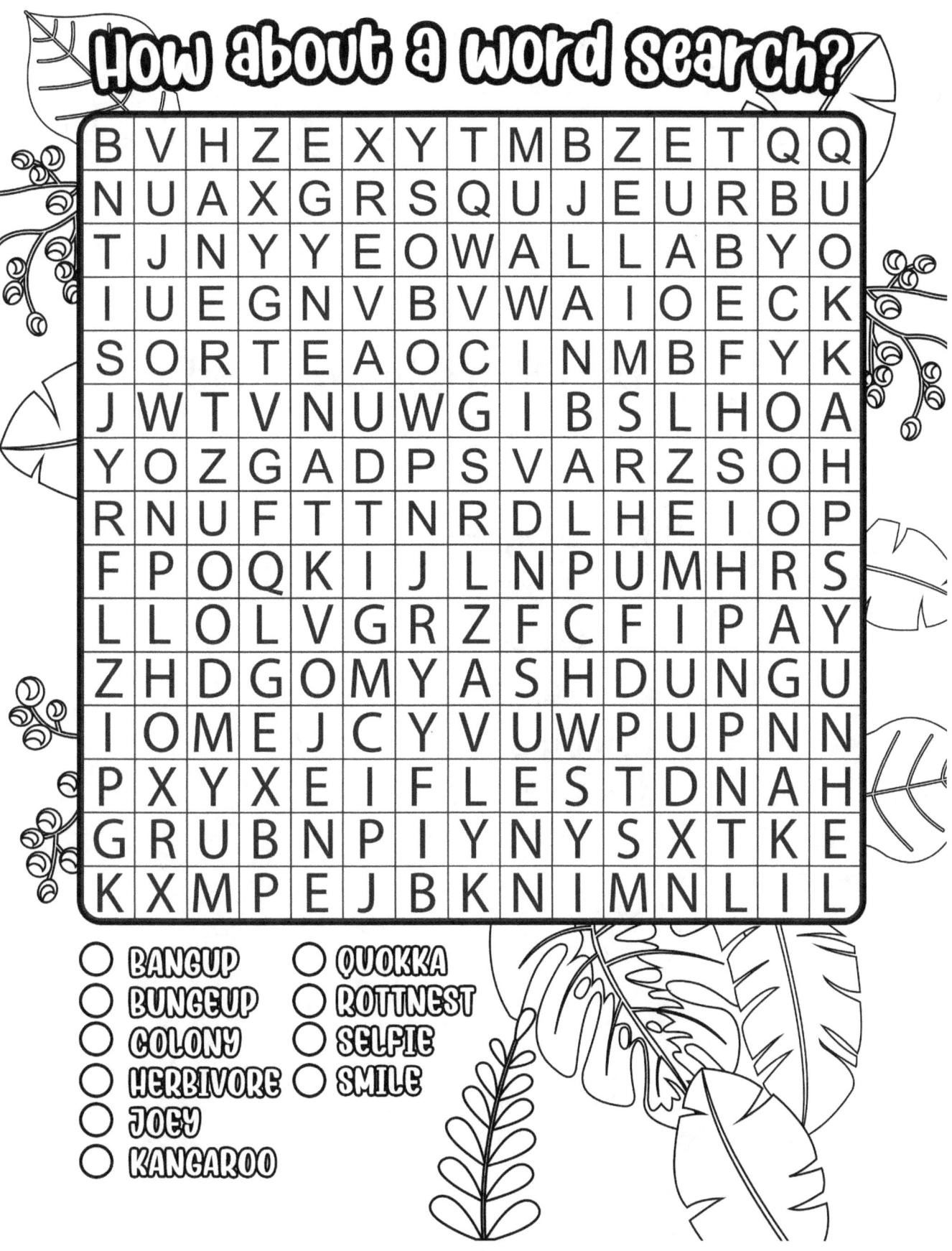

```
B V H Z E X Y T M B Z E T Q Q
N U A X G R S Q U J E U R B U
T J N Y Y E O W A L L A B Y O
I U E G N V B V W A I O E C K
S O R T E A O C I N M B F Y K
J W T V N U W G I B S L H O A
Y O Z G A D P S V A R Z S O H
R N U F T T N R D L H E I O P
F P O Q K I J L N P U M H R S
L L O L V G R Z F C F I P A Y
Z H D G O M Y A S H D U N G U
I O M E J C Y V U W P U P N N
P X Y X E I F L E S T D N A H
G R U B N P I Y N Y S X T K E
K X M P E J B K N I M N L I L
```

- ○ BANGUP
- ○ BUNGEUP
- ○ COLONY
- ○ HERBIVORE
- ○ JOEY
- ○ KANGAROO
- ○ QUOKKA
- ○ ROTTNEST
- ○ SELFIE
- ○ SMILE

Let's try a color-by-letter!

A. Orange
B. Brown
C. Green
D. Purple
E. Blue
F. Red

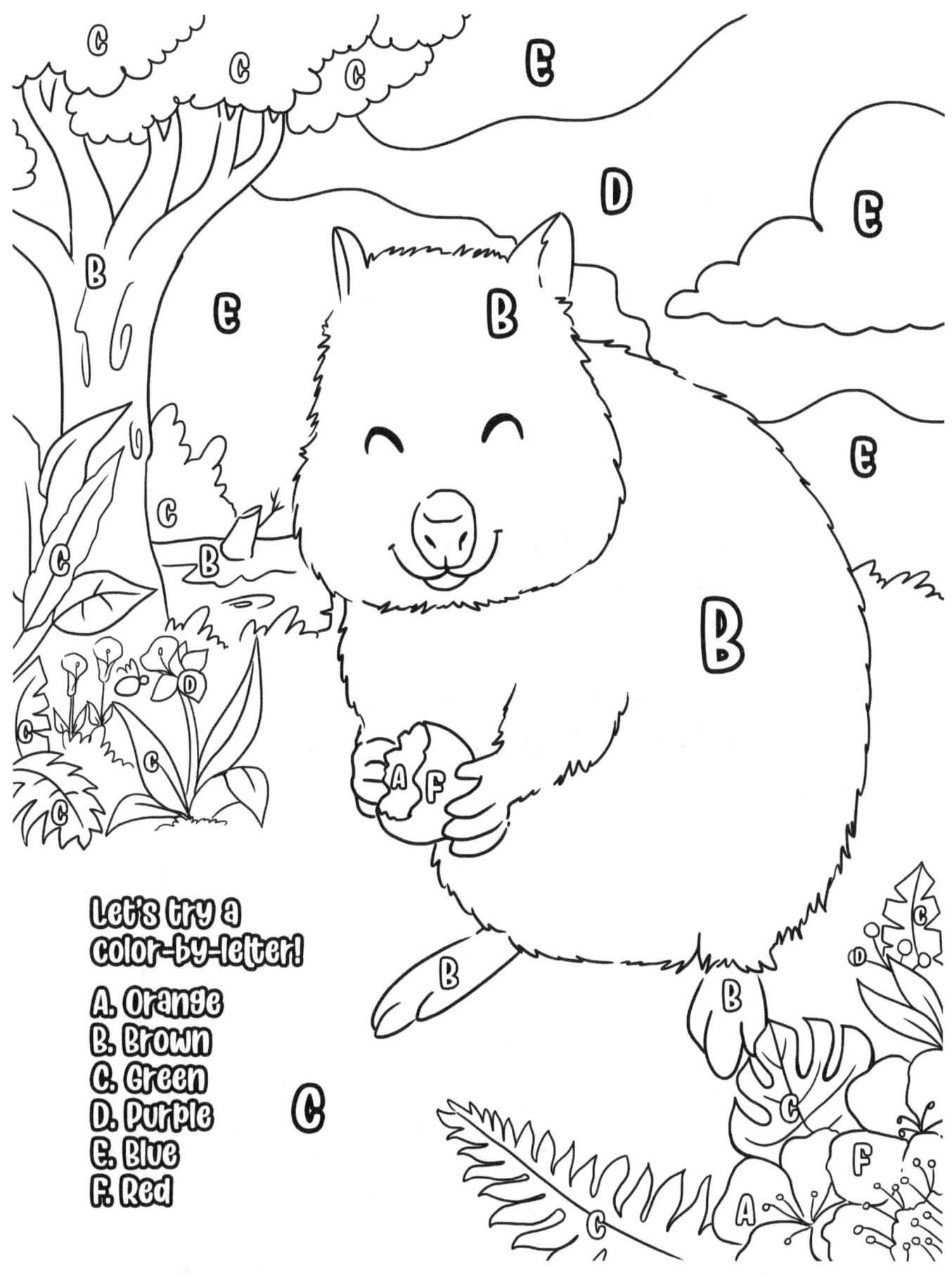

Let's try a
color-by-letter!

A. Orange
B. Brown
C. Green
D. Purple
E. Blue
F. Red

What is a marsupial's favorite soft-drink?

Quokka-Koala! (Try saying it in a Brooklyn accent if you're not sure!)

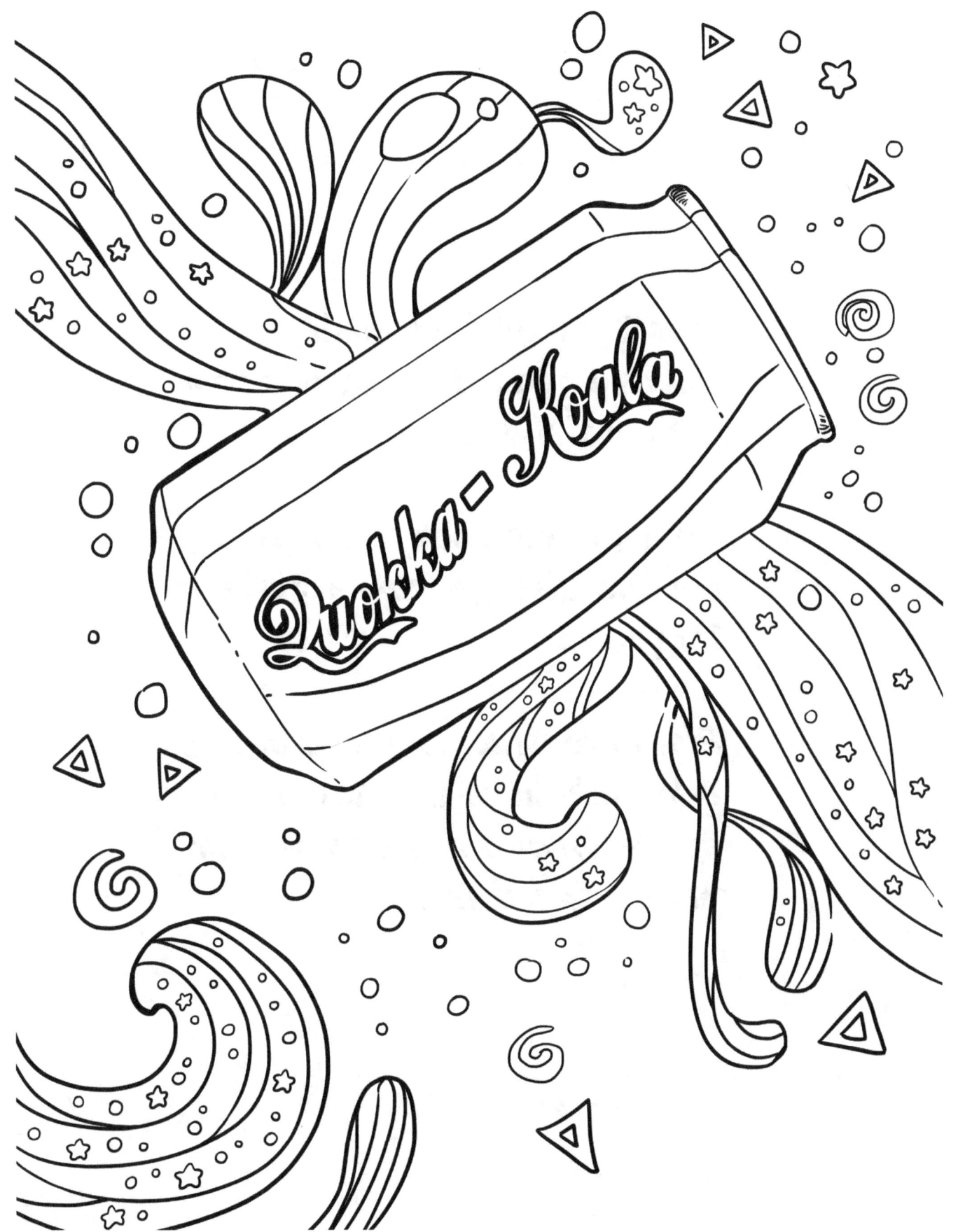

Aren't you glad we made a coloring book about quokkas and not quokka-diles?

We hope this book has been a not-too-*questionable* experience for you!

Please consider checking out our other educational coloring books and leaving us a review at your place of purchase.

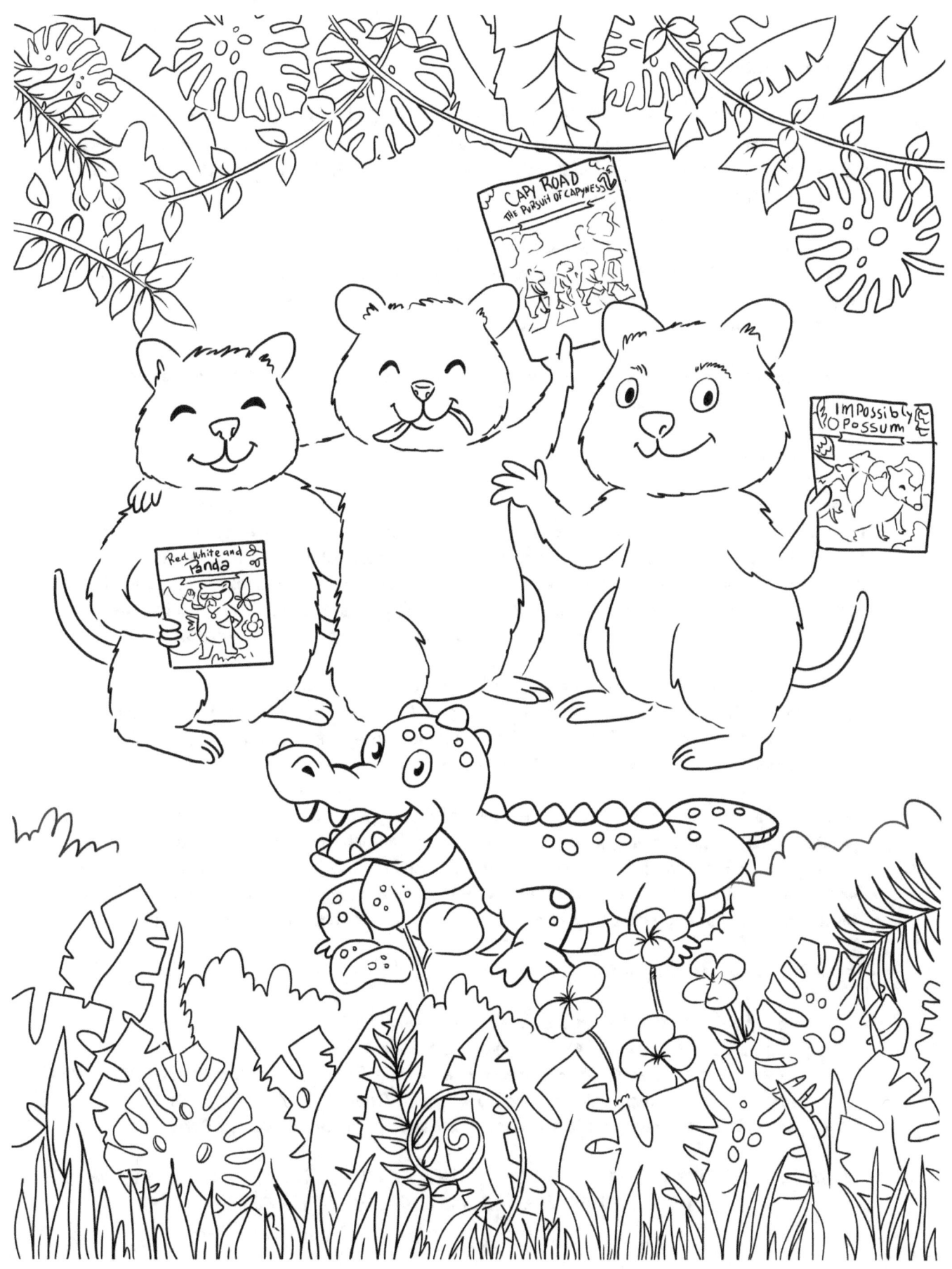

About the Editor

Jonathan Terry, DO, ABIHM, IFMCP is a board-certified osteopathic physician and surgeon, a general psychiatrist, a Diplomate of the American Board of Psychiatry and Neurology (ABPN), a Diplomate of the National Board of Physicians and Surgeons (NBPAS), and a Diplomate of the American Board of Integrative Holistic Medicine (ABIHM). He serves on faculty in several accredited medical schools, residency programs, and professional training programs. Dr. Terry is proud to be a National Health Service Corps Ambassador and works primarily with underserved populations, high-acuity inpatient psychiatric patients, and in consultation for program and policy-building initiatives. Dr. Terry's clinical interests include primary care consultation, nutrition, osteopathy, integrative medicine, kindness, and prevention.

Read more at www.DrJonathanTerry.com, and follow us on Facebook @MyCapybara and @DrJonathanTerry. Dr. Jonathan Terry is also on YouTube.

About the Book

Questionable Quokkas is about community investment and involvement at every level. International artists from underserved areas were independently interviewed and contracted as contributors to enthusiastically craft this unique, memorable collection while providing investment in their local communities. Proceeds from the book are reinvested in mental health initiatives including prevention, education, and providing free or discounted care to those without insurance, those who cannot access care, students, and impaired professionals.

We're especially proud to feature licensed artwork from *Desiree Albarran* from Bogotá, Colombia. Desiree likes to draw with all possible materials and techniques, making many funny characters that people love. She is a cat lover, cookie hunter, and assiduous gamer. See Desiree's portfolio at: https://www.behance.net/desireeart.

We've once again enlisted the help of our Layout Editor, pun artist extraordinaire, and principal quokka researcher, Sarah Mugridge. As a true Californian, when she isn't writing quokka coloring books Sarah can be found soaking up the sunshine outdoors, growing cool plants in her garden, and baking tasty treats! We'd also like to extend a special thanks to Terry Geldres-Becerra for contributing some very *questionable* quokka facts and puns. What a quok of fun!

Check Out Our Other Colorful Titles:

- *Eat The Rainbow* & the *Eat the Rainbow Coloring Book*
- *The Pursuit of Capyness: A Zen Capybara Coloring Book*
- *Red, White, and Panda: An Educational Red Panda Coloring Book for Adults and Children*
- *Impossibly Opossum: Coloring Book, Facts, and Games!*
- *Capy Road: The Pursuit of Capyness 2 – A Happier Capybara Coloring Book*

IF YOU LIKE THIS BOOK, PLEASE LEAVE US A REVIEW AT YOUR PURCHASE SITE! REVIEWS ARE SO IMPORTANT FOR HELPING THIS BOOK HELP OTHER PEOPLE